DEMOCRACY

FOR BEGINNERS®

DEMOCRACY
FOR BEGINNERS®

BY **ROBERT CAVALIER**

ILLUSTRATIONS BY **REUBEN NEGRÓN**

FOR BEGINNERS®

an imprint of Steerforth Press
Hanover, New Hampshire

For Beginners LLC
62 East Starrs Plain Road
Danbury, CT 06810 USA
www.forbeginnersbooks.com

A For Beginners® Documentary Comic Book
Copyright © 2009

Cataloging-in-Publication information is available from the Library of Congress.

ISBN # 978-1-934389-36-2 Trade

Manufactured in the United States of America

For Beginners® and Beginners Documentary Comic Books® are published
by For Beginners LLC.

First Edition

10 9 8 7 6 5 4 3 2 1

Can you tell a book by its cover?

Pericles represents Athenian *direct democracy* (all citizens directly participate in the government) and Thomas Jefferson represents American *representative democracy* (citizens elect people to represent them in the government). America's democratic institutions rely on a separation of powers, divided into a legislative branch (House and Senate) and executive branch (President) along with an independent judiciary (like the Supreme Court). Other democracies have, for example, a parliamentary form of government similar to that found in Britain. Here the executive is dependent on the legislature and can be removed through a vote of confidence.

The building between Pericles and Jefferson is our Capitol dome. It reflects the architecture of ancient Greece and Rome, evoking republican ideals that guided our nation's founders.

For most of history, it was men, white men, who could vote and make decisions. Over time—too much time—citizen rights were expanded to include non-whites and women. This more inclusive sense of democracy is seen in the image of a town hall meeting, where "suffrage" (from the Latin *suffragium*, meaning "voting tablet") has been made universal.

By the way, most of us think that voting is the key element of democratic institutions. But it's also important to see what goes on before voting—and how this affects our understanding of citizenship. One theory that looks at this is called *deliberative democracy*.

There's a lot happening on the cover—let's see what's inside!

Table of Contents

Preface: Understanding Democracy

With all the talk about "democracy" these days, it's surprising how little time is spent thinking about *the very idea* of democracy—the *history* of this political institution and the *justification* for it as a political institution.

In this book we'll look at the history and concept of democracy as well as some challenges that democracy faces today. And while we focus on the American institution of democracy, much of what we say can be applied more broadly.

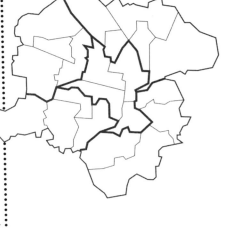

But first a little quiz.

- What state district do you live in?
- Who is your state senator?
- If you live in a city, who is your city council person?
- What ward do you live in? What is a "ward"? (This was a big deal for Thomas Jefferson.)
- If you're old enough, when was the last time you voted in a presidential election?
- Have you ever attended a community meeting?
- Have you ever contacted any of your city and state representatives?

Don't feel bad if you didn't do well on this test, most Americans don't. One reason for reading this book is to see how we all can be better at this—better at doing democracy.

By the way, for Thomas Jefferson, to ensure a properly educated citizenry, you should "divide every county into wards of five or six miles square..." (letter to John Adams, 1813). Why? Because it was here, in the wards, that our education would begin. And education counts!

Thomas Jefferson

"I know no safe depositary of the ultimate powers of the society but the people themselves; and if we think them not enlightened enough to exercise their control with a wholesome discretion, the remedy is not to take it from them, but to inform their discretion by education. This is the true corrective of abuses of constitutional power."
–letter to W. Jarvis, 1820

In the Beginning

Most people see democracy or "rule by the people" as having its origins in the Greek city-state (*polis*). Over many decades during the 6th and 5th centuries B.C.E.*, Greek society evolved from a culture of powerful warlords to a culture of laws and law-givers.

In **Athens**, new laws divided the country into "demes" or grids, and Athenian citizens became numerical entities—equal to each other in their ability to cast votes and influence policy. Of course, these citizens were males born in Athens; the larger majority of those living in Athens—women, slaves, and resident foreigners—had no voice in the city.

Still, without being too rosy-eyed, it was a remarkable achievement. By the mid-5th century, during the Age of Pericles, the city-state of Athens had become the world's first fully functioning, direct, participatory democracy. As **Pericles** himself once famously said:

> *"Our constitution ... favors the many instead of the few; this is why it is called a democracy. If we look to the laws, they afford equal justice to all in their private differences; if to social standing, advancement in public life falls to reputation for capacity, class considerations not being allowed to interfere with merit; nor again does poverty bar the way, if a man is able to serve the state, he is not hindered by the obscurity of his condition...."*

* "Before the Common Era" is what historians formerly called "Before Christ" (B.C.)

PERICLES

3

Pericles' oration came from a funeral speech given during a disastrous war between Athens and Sparta. By the end of the century, Athens would recover little of its former glory—and when democracy was restored after a brief period of Spartan-supported tyranny, the Athenians set about to bring one of its most notorious citizens, Socrates, to trial on charges of impiety and corruption of the youth. (Many saw Socrates—as some see secularism today—as a corrupting influence and the source for many of the ills that beset the state.)

Whipping up the emotions of the jurors—some 501 of them—Socrates' accusers eventually convicted him of these charges—and the penalty was death by hemlock.

SOCRATES

The philosopher **Plato** (429-347 B.C.E.) was present during this ordeal and would later come to be one of the greatest critics of democratic institutions.

4

For Plato, the trial and death of Socrates was proof that the voice of the people is easily shaped and often mistaken. The masses are the *last* people to be put in power.

> *You wouldn't turn to a rowdy crew to pilot a ship across difficult waters…you'd turn to the captain of the ship, whose expert knowledge would always outweigh the opinion of the many.*

PLATO

Appealing to the people (those feisty *hoi poloi*) becomes the *ad populum* fallacy—if everyone thinks the earth is flat, this doesn't mean that the earth *is* flat. Of every statement of the form, "The people say X is good," we can always ask, "But *is* it good?"—and an answer to that requires a separate investigation. We ultimately want knowledge of these matters, not mere opinion…or opinion polls.

For Plato, such knowledge is ultimately found in a separate realm of eternal ideas (of justice, goodness, and beauty). And only those statesmen who are capable of understanding these ideas could truly be political leaders. This is his ideal of the philosopher-king. A truly bad idea, as the philosopher Karl Popper might say.

Aristotle (384-322 B.C.E.), the other great philosopher of the Classical Period, also had grave misgivings about democracy. In his discussions of the different types of constitutions found in the Ancient world, Aristotle believed that democracy would be beset by the class problems of rich and poor—and that the people will think of themselves and not the common good. This would lead, he feared, to mob rule and a tyranny of the majority.

ARISTOTLE

Actually, it's more complicated for Aristotle. There are two forms of "rule by many"—one includes everybody (the crowd), the other is limited to rule by property owners. The ancients (and some of our Founding Fathers) felt that property owners would have more of a stake in the order of society and could not easily be bought off (as the very poor might).

Aristotle also perceived that a rising middle class of merchants would also have a moderating effect on democracies.

Still, for much of history, democracies of any kind were seen as inferior to regimes run by good monarchs (rule by one) or by aristocracies (rule by a few, the best, the *aristos*). These kinds of good rulers would supposedly be guided by virtue, seeking peace and the Common Good for all.*

---

* Aristotle also listed deficient versions of "rule by one" and "rule by many." These were called tyrannies and oligarchies (a few of the wealthy): both tyrants and oligarchs rule for the sake of themselves, not for the good of the country.

For these early critics, democracy as a political institution doesn't really help us answer the question: What ought we, as a society, to do?

Seen as a decision-procedure, democracy seems to put the wrong people (the majority) in charge, since they lack:

(a) sufficient knowledge (Plato) and

(b) sufficient goodness (Aristotle).

By the way, the Greek idea of a city-state also saddled the concept of democracy with the notion that for everyone to participate in self-government, they would have to show up at meetings. For Aristotle a political state should be no larger than a three-day walk from the center.

Hence direct, participatory democracies would seem to be limited in size (Swiss cantons and New England towns). Yet again, as far as making decisions is concerned, size really doesn't matter—either way, it's still a bad idea to take a vote.

No sooner had Aristotle finished his philosophy than the world of the Greek city-state began to come to an end. **Alexander the Great** (who, as Alexander the Boy, was tutored by Aristotle) had conquered the world—all the way to India and down to Alexandria (in ancient Egypt).

ALEXANDER THE GREAT

After Alexander's death, his empire was divided into large kingdoms and soon after there arose in the West (Italy) a new force in the ancient world: the Romans.

As Rome ascended, it developed its own idea of a republic and quickly expanded its empire to rule the world. A culture of engineers and military legions, it also gave rise to thinkers like **Cicero** (106 - 43 B.C.E.), who literally and figuratively translated Greek philosophy into latin.

CICERO

Following Aristotle's division of constitutions (rule by one, the few, and the many), he noted that the absolute rule of a wise king might be best, but succession makes this regime unstable, the first and most certain to decay. Even a great ruler can beget a lousy son.

So Cicero advocated a *mixed constitution* consisting of consuls (executive, royal power), senate (aristocratic, deliberative power), and tribunes (representing the interests of the "plebs" or the people).

This scheme actually anticipates elements of our own democracy—corresponding roughly to our President, Senate, and House of Representatives. In this regard, John Adams, for one, took his study of Cicero seriously. He relied on the Roman philosopher and statesman for his arguments in favor of a democracy divided into separate branches of government. In *A Defense of the Constitutions of Government of the United States of America* (1787), this division involves what we call a strong executive branch, a "bicameral" legislature (the two *camera*, Latin for "chambers," of Senate and House) and an independent judiciary.

Bravo for mixed constitutions!

John Adams

A Word About Virtue

For the ancients, much was made about the cultivation of human excellence (that was the original meaning of virtue for the Greeks). We all want to be excellent, don't we?

In one's relations to the self and others, one can achieve a kind of excellence by cultivating certain moral and intellectual virtues (e.g., courage, interest in literature).

There are also virtues involved in household management (e.g., raising a family, paying bills).

Finally, there are the virtues of a citizen partaking in the life of the city. Our Founding Fathers were greatly impressed with the Roman understanding of civic virtue as were they of the Stoic ideals that saw everyone partaking of a universal reason and a natural law theory that proclaimed the universality of justice.

But the ideals of the republic collapsed with the rise the Caesars (a.k.a. dictators). Cicero himself was murdered under one of the Roman regimes, his head put on a stick where the orators spoke (this was when politics was really rough!).

Yet as Athens gave way to Rome, so too Rome to Jerusalem…. At first persecuted, the early Christians slowly won the respect of Roman emperors and Rome itself, though much diminished, eventually became the Holy Roman Empire.

Writing his great work, *The City of God*, as the barbarians were at the gates of his North African town, **Augustine** (354—430 C.E.) tried to combine Platonic ideas with Christian ideals. The good news of the New Testament was that there is a personal God who knows our thoughts and deeds and guides us toward a certain kind of life unknown to the pagan world and unattainable by pagan philosophy.

> *"We see then that the two cities were created by two kinds of love: The earthly city was created by self-love reaching the point of contempt for God, the Heavenly City by the love of God carried as far as contempt of self."*
> —*The City of God*
> (Book XIV)

Augustine adopted the ancient idea that a goal of State is to provide peace and that true leaders and citizens always think of the common good of all rather than their own good: "The virtue that characterizes the citizen as citizen and orders all citizens to the end or *common good* of the city is justice.... By regulating relations among men it preserves peace [for] ... without peace ... no society can prosper or even subsist."

He now adds to this a foundation for universal justice lacking even in the ideals of the Stoics: *Temporal laws* serve all who live in earthly cities but an *eternal law* also exists to guide and justify those who also choose to live in the City of God whilst living on earth.

These different laws will be further investigated by Thomas Aquinas in his famous Natural Law theory.

By the way, it's here that we can start to see the origins of contemporary debates over the foundations of our American Constitution. Is it a human law or is it based upon an eternal, God-given law?

Islamic Perspectives

When the Western Roman Empire collapsed, the empires to the East continued. The Byzantium empire, for example, had its seat in Constantinople (today's Istanbul, Turkey). And while the West fell into the Dark Ages (not much writing, Rome went to pasture), the East maintained its culture and many of the writings of the past (including the works of the Plato and Aristotle).

Around 600 C.E. a remarkable new religion appeared, with the prophet Muhammad succeeding the prophets Abraham and Jesus (today we speak of this as the Abrahamic Tradition referring to the Jewish, Christian, and Islamic faiths). Within a few decades after his death in 632 C.E., Islam had spread across the East and soon approached Spain to the west.

This period has also been known for its high culture, which included art, mathematics, and philosophy. Of particular interest today are the writings of **Alfarabi** (c. 870-950 C.E.). Like Augustine before him, he sought to harmonize his faith with the ideas of the Greek philosophers.

Alfarabi

Alfarabi examined the relation between Plato's "Best Regime" and the Divine Law of Islam. He imagined Philosopher-Kings and Prophet-Legislators. In his utopia "the virtuous regime is a nonhereditary monarchical or an aristocratic regime in which the best rule." Its citizens are virtuous and knowledgeable and act in accord with this knowledge (of divine and natural beings and that which brings about true human happiness).

But he was enough of a realist to understand that such a regime may not come into being. So he looked for a second-best regime and, surprisingly, it was a democratic regime. Why?

For Alfarabi, a democracy may be messy and contain many vices (as people are pretty free to do and say what they want), but it is tolerant and would therefore allow Muslims to be Muslims and practice their religion. It also has the best chance—or rather second best chance—to allow for the cultivation of the Arts and Sciences (as it will no doubt contain people interested in those sorts of activities as well).

So there is, within the very tradition of Islam, a positive view of democracy. This is good news.

The Dark Ages in the West were not completely dark. Writing had gone on in monasteries and eventually feudal kingdoms appeared—as the outlines of an early Europe began to take shape. The building of monumental cathedrals gave temporal presence to the dominance of Christianity at this time and soon these cathedrals gave rise to the first universities (for example: Oxford, Notre Dame, and Bologna).

Thomas Aquinas (1225-1274) was a theologian at the University of Paris. His political philosophy is similar to that of the Greeks and Romans, with the addition of Christian beliefs: An ideal city is one ruled absolutely by a single wise man for the sake of virtue. But a second-best society is a well ordered, mixed regime whose human laws do not conflict with natural law: It combines the best elements of monarchy (wise ruler), aristocracy (wise legislators), and polity (consent of the ruled).

Aquinas expands upon the earlier concepts of *Natural Law*, developing four kinds of laws that govern all things in one way or another:

Eternal Law is the overarching order of the entire universe that governs the physical and moral universe (and that is grounded in the will and wisdom of God).

Natural Law is that aspect of eternal law that pertains to morality and human behavior. It prescribes the fundamental precepts of morality and is grasped through practical reason and conscience.

Human Law pertains to the local laws of cities and states. It can vary from place to place (traffic laws, tax laws), but can never violate Natural Law.

Divine Law exhorts inner justice and guarantees just rewards and punishments in the afterlife. It can only be discovered through revelation. The Bible is one way this is revealed to us—telling us that we are saved, that there will be a final judgment, etc.

Consequences of the Natural Law Theory of Aquinas

While Natural Law theory had its origins with the Stoics, Augustine was able to advance upon the pagans by grounding Natural Law in the Christian God. In Aquinas, these Natural Laws become canonical (not canons, but *rules*).

Here are some of them:

- Help one another and avoid harming others.
- Preserve one's life.
- Extend the life of the species (procreate).

The kinds of rules that Natural Law prescribes are very, very general ...but they have been interpreted in ways that have far-reaching consequences for our society today.

It makes sense to want to preserve our lives. But what if at the end of our natural lives we wish to shorten the pain and suffering by some form of physician assisted suicide? Our state laws cannot allow this, because in doing so, these Human Laws would be violating Natural Law.

By prohibiting conception, birth control pills and other forms of contraceptives also violate Natural Law.

What about homosexuality? The very practice of homosexuality violates Natural Law because procreation is impossible. Any Human Laws that allow for, say, same-sex marriage, would thereby violate Natural Law.

You can see how Thomism is still with us in contemporary debates over social values issues.

But just as Aristotle's notion of the city-state underwent significant revision shortly after his passing, Natural Law theory would also change in the upcoming centuries—as would the whole period that gave rise to it.

The **Renaissance** (14th-16th centuries) saw a new birth in the arts and sciences as trade and printing brought a new era to the West. The medieval mind was giving way to the modern world.

Some of the most earth-shaking events took place in the sciences, in astronomy and physics.

By reversing the view of the earth as the center of the universe, Copernicus not only put the Sun at the center, but for some he took away our sense of being special (the center of attention). We were becoming a speck of dust floating about a meaningless universe.

COPERNICUS (1473-1543)   GALILEO (1564-1642)

Things didn't get better when Galileo challenged Aristotle's ideas about the physics of motion. Along the way, he observed moons around Jupiter...something that should not have been (there was a reason why there were seven planets—it was part of God's ordering of things)...but if those moons existed, then God may *not* exist! Our whole moral universe was a risk!

This is the old tension between science and religion. We see it played out today in debates over Darwinism in high school curriculum. We also see it played out when talking about the foundations of our constitution—if there were no God, no trans-empirical ground for our democratic institution, would that render our democracy meaningless?

Machiavelli (1469-1527) didn't make things any better:

> "Since my intention is to say something that will prove of practical use to the inquirer, I have thought it proper to represent things as they are in real truth, rather than as they are imagined. Many have dreamed up republics and principalities which have never in truth been known to exist; the gulf between how one should live and how one does live is so wide that a man who neglects what is actually done for what should be done learns the way of self-destruction rather than self-preservation. The fact that a man who wants to act virtuously in every way necessarily comes to grief among so many who are not virtuous. Therefore if a prince wants to maintain his rule he must learn how not to be virtuous, and to make use of this or not according to need."
> —The Prince

NICCOLO MACCHIAVELLI

Plato, Cicero, Augustine—all previous writers on political philosophy—told us how things *ought* to be...they wrote utopias. Machiavelli tells his prince how to rule in accordance with the way things *really* are.

In the real, Machiavellian world, rulers survive and states become stable when things are done in any way that gets the job done. As a ruler, your real virtue is to know how to do this—how to be virtuous if it serves your needs and how to be deceitful, manipulative, and vicious when that serves your needs. Of course, you can't be a cruel tyrant—nor do you want the people to love you (that's too fickle)...a healthy respect for your power and deeds will be enough.

17

Behind this is the rather unhealthy idea that in politics anything will do as long as it gets you elected or keeps you elected. It leads to media campaigns that seek to manipulate the voter and influence the outcome at whatever cost.

But one person's realism is another person's cynicism. We'll come back to this....

Reformation

In 1517 **Martin Luther** (1483-1546) published his "95 Theses." These decrees were the outcome of years of anger and frustration over what he felt were the excesses of his Catholic Church. He was particularly upset over the sale of indulgences—exchanges of time off in purgatory and amnesty for one's sins—for amounts of money to be used for, among other things, the growing costs of Vatican renovation and expansion.

There was also a healthy business in relics ranging from splinters of the cross to vials of saints' blood to bits and pieces of the Apostles' bones and hair. The trade was so big that it seemed that of the Twelve Apostles, 28 of them must have been buried in Germany!

He reacted to all this by declaring that simple faith replaces the power of the papacy.

The local princes and nobles liked the sound of this, because so much of their land belonged to the Catholic Church. If faith and the bible were all we needed, then let's split from the Church and take back the land as well. These kinds of unintended consequences multiplied and soon all kinds of religious sects arose. The reformation turned into revolution as real world politics confronted the once universal (*catholos*) Church.

Against Luther's wishes, the specter of religious wars soon covered Europe. The *St. Bartholomew Massacre* in 1572 showed the world the violence that man can visit upon man in times of civil unrest.

As horrible as it was, it also showed what happens to society once it breaks down. And it showed thinkers like **Thomas Hobbes** (1588-1679), in particular, what a State of Nature must look like.

His *Leviathan* (1651) became the first attempt at what we call political science. Taking a cue from the New Science, Hobbes sought to explain 'human motion' as Galileo had used his science to explain physical motion.

Hobbes's observation of human beings in civil and religious warfare led him to see how the collapse of society reveals a State of Nature as "war of all against all" in which life is "beastly, brutal, and short." Our true nature is also seen in this condition.

It's a dismal picture. Our nature is revealed in our passions (hope for glory, fear of death) and our lives are reduced to one Natural Law: Self-preservation.

Self-interest becomes our guiding principle—and also our saving grace. For it is self-interest, working with reason, that shows us a way out of the State of Nature.

Take any civil war or natural disaster and let society collapse. Sooner than you'd think, people would start to pile up food, then protect their stash. Guns and other weapons would come out.

Yet even the strongest out there would need to sleep and could easily be killed while dreaming. In this sense, we are all equal.

Thankfully, we can also see the need to escape this State of Nature (because it is in our self-interest to do so) and we do this by transferring our individual powers to a state (Leviathan) that will in turn act to protect us.

In a sense, we contract with a state (be it a democracy, aristocracy, or monarchy) and say, OK, you protect me and my property and I'll obey your laws since they help bring about peace.

Something like this often happens when, for example, a society collapses into anarchy. One of the first things people do is create a constitution that brings into being a new Civil Authority with its law and order. And as there was a lot of talk during Hobbes' time of contracts and contract theory, he used this notion to describe what we call a *Social Contract*.

In the history of democracy, Locke's *Two Treatises on Government* (1690) stands at the crossroads. While Hobbes considered democracy an option for his Leviathan, he traditionally opted for a strong monarchy (with its ability to make quick decisions). Hobbes even hoped the kings would like him for this, which they didn't. **John Locke** (1632-1704) was different.

His First Treatise was an attack Robert Filmer's defense of the Divine Right of kings. The idea that kings could trace their bloodlines to Adam was foolish, Locke wrote, and in no way gave them any superiority to other men. People are not divided into those with "blue blood" and those who are commoners. Indeed, in the Second Treatise, we get a new take on Natural Law that declares all men free and equal. Locke's words also anticipate an earlier version of our Declaration of Independence, which spoke of "life, liberty and property." For Locke—

"The natural liberty of man is ... to have only the law of nature for his rule...and reason, which is that law, teaches all mankind...that...no one ought to harm another in his life, health, liberty or possessions...."

Thomas Jefferson memorialized these sentiments in the Declaration of Independence:

"We hold these truths to be self-evident, that all men are created equal, that they are endowed by their Creator with certain unalienable Rights, that among these are Life, Liberty and the pursuit of Happiness...."

Note that the change from "property" to the wider meaning of "pursuit of happiness" is profound; just as an editorial change from "sacred and undeniable" in the first draft to "self-evident" in the final draft is powerful.

Locke also came up with another version of the social contract, this time arising from the inconviences of a State of Nature. In his State of Nature each person has to watch out for his or her own goods and properties (such goods arising out of their labor—their hands mixing with nature to produce property—like canned apple sauce from an abundant apple tree grove).

Now, Locke's State of Nature is a kinder and gentler one than that of Hobbes, but we nevertheless feel the need to enter into a Civil Society to protect our property (estate) from being taken over by arbitrary power (of those stronger than ourselves, etc.). More than that, we ourselves need protection of our most valuable assets—our life and liberty!

In this, Locke anticipated Immanuel Kant (1724-1804), who viewed human life as intrinsically valuable, as possessing dignity. We are ends-in-ourselves and can never be reduced to mere means only (as serfs in France and slaves in America were).

Immanuel Kant

Locke's Second Treatise also gave a modern context to earlier versions of mixed constitutions by designing a representational government with Executive and Legislative branches. He also suggested that if kings proceed with arbitrary and systematic violation of Natural Law, then there is a right to revolution. As we'll see, this latter argument was used in America's Declaration of Independence.

By the way, Locke felt that a political solution to religious wars was to be found in the idea of religious toleration. Soon Toleration Acts appeared around the world and guaranteed religious freedom or freedom of conscience, at least as long as you weren't too much of a nonconformist. Atheists were often considered beyond the pale. They still are today, at least for offices like the President of the United States.

Hobbes, Locke, and
The Negative Liberal Tradition

Let's look at what Hobbes and Locke have to do with our modern notions of democracy. Both look at our pre-political life as a key to understanding our actual political life—that's the role of the state of nature. Both also talk of the individual as contracting out of this state of nature into a civil society (a state with a certain form of government).

For Hobbes, what we seek is freedom *from* (i.e., negative freedom) interference by other persons. Though the Leviathan/ state can *coerce* me e.g., force me to follow the rules of civil society and punish me if I don't, the state also *protects* me from a life that is 'beastly, brutal, and short.'

For Locke, what we seek is freedom *from* interference with our natural rights (to life, liberty, and estate/property). The state protects us from, e.g., theft and tyranny (it can punish those who do such things and enforce contracts, etc.).

Now while Hobbes remained loyal to monarchy, Locke emphasized the moral significance of liberty and equality—and these moral attributes of being human are explicitly granted by "democratic constitutions."

Historically, this notion of "freedom from" emphasizes the freedom of the individual from intrusions by the state. The state is there to protect by life and property, but its role should be limited in other respects. This is the beginning of the classical liberal tradition, a tradition that emphasizes individual liberty and small government. It is the tradition that Thomas Paine embodies when he writes:

"Every man wishes to pursue his occupation, and to enjoy the fruits of his labors and the produce of his property, and with the least possible expense. When these things are accomplished, all the objects for which government ought to be established are answered."

Thomas Paine

Jean-Jacque Rousseau

Jean-Jacques Rousseau (1712-1778) offers another and radically different social contract theory. He's French, so why not be contrarian?

In his *state of nature*, men and women enjoy idleness and the pleasure of their own existence, just like the idyllic paintings of South Sea Islanders. This "pre-political person" has a natural sympathy for the suffering of others, but also a sense of perfectibility along with the natural desire to preserve himself.

25

All goes well until some start to say "this belongs to me" and sympathy is replaced by self-interest. Contrary to Locke's view, for Rousseau this origin of property is the beginning of the end—it is the origin of "inequality." At some point those with property suggest a contract to form civil society, thus ensuring that this inequality becomes legalized. How different civil man is from natural man!

Once we've left the state of nature, we can't return—but we can improve things by establishing a just civil society, a moral society with binding commitments to others.

How do we do this? By coming together as a community (Rousseau had in mind something like the small Swiss cantons) and legislating laws that not only protect property, but also the rights of the people. He imagined citizens coming together to say "this is how *we* wish to be governed, this is what *we* ought to do." Whenever a new constitution is formed, it is formed this way. Whenever a constitution is amended, it is amended this way.

An individual's contract with society not only concerns the individual alone, but the individual as a citizen. And when one acts as a citizen, Rousseau argued, one is truly free (i.e., even though one may not *want* to pay taxes, one does because it is their *duty* as a citizen to do so—in a sense, individuals give themselves laws that in turn they follow).

Historically, this notion of self-legislation (autonomy) has been called "positive freedom." For Rousseau it is connected to the idea of a General Will and can be seen in a constitutional convention in which individual participants agree to adopt only what all could will (e.g., a liberal democratic constitution). A government formed by such a democratic constitution must be powerful enough to rule over the particular wills of its citizens (e.g., levy taxes), but not powerful enough to dominate the General Will or the laws based upon it (i.e., change the constitution or violate the laws of the land as some democratically elected leaders sometimes try to do).

If he had left things like this, perhaps we could follow him. But while Rousseau spoke glowingly of human dignity and the virtues of choosing the general will over the private, he also spoke of the need for society to educate or punish those who stray by "forcing them to be free." The early history of the French Revolution with its people's courts and Reign of Terror soon provided examples of regimes that would make a mockery of these ideas.

The Reign of Terror - France (1793-1794)

Whether this is a criticism of Rousseau or a caricature is open to debate. But for whatever reason, Rousseau's ideas have been a focus of 20th-century political discussions ever since the publication of Isaiah Berlin's "Two Concepts of Liberty." Here, Berlin sides with the notion of negative liberty and argues that the concept of positive liberty leads to totalitarian regimes like that found in the former Soviet Union. Individuals are crushed under the General Will (or the British Labor Party).

The American Revolt Against King George

We'll come back to the concepts of negative and positive liberty when we look at the scope and limits of the modern liberal state. The origins of this state, by the way, were moving from theory to practice in 18th-century revolutions against political monarchies.

In 1765 the British Parliament imposed a **Stamp Act** requiring that all manner of goods carry a stamp, the cost of which was a tax upon members of the American colonies. Since this order came from Britain without consultation or approval by local colonial legislatures, it was seen as *taxation without represen-tation*. Colonial resentment against British rule began to boil.

Taxes were also imposed at ports and on goods brought into those ports. For the most part, this was normal business. However, in 1773 the British government passed a **Tea Act**, which allowed Britain's East India Company to sell tea to the colonies at greatly reduced prices, thereby undercutting prices offered by local colonial merchants and those who smuggled goods into the colonies (one of these "smugglers" was John Hancock). A protest against this move by the British Parliament became known as The Boston Tea Party.

After these kinds of protests in Boston, the British sent combat troops. In 1775 fight-ing broke out in Lexington and Concord and the **American Revolutionary War** had begun.

The Rights of Man

The ideas of human dignity and human rights gained currency in the period called The Enlightenment and were the moral background of the French and American revolutions. The struggles in the American colonies leading up to the break with King George were a reflection of this and are echoed in our **Declaration of Independence** (parts of which we've stated):

> *"We hold these truths to be self-evident, that all men are created equal, that they are endowed by their Creator with certain unalienable Rights, that among these are Life, Liberty and the pursuit of Happiness. —That to secure these rights, Governments are instituted among Men, deriving their just powers from the consent of the governed, —That whenever any Form of Government becomes destructive of these ends, it is the Right of the People to alter or to abolish it, and to institute new Government, laying its foundation on such principles and organizing its powers in such form, as to them shall seem most likely to effect their Safety and Happiness...."*
>
> *(July 4, 1776)*

"What do we mean by the American Revolution? Do we mean the American war? The Revolution was effected before the war commenced. The Revolution was in the minds and hearts of the people.... This radical change in the principles, opinions, sentiments, and affections of the people was the real American Revolution." —John Adams

John Adams

29

Property and Commerce

Other ideas from the 17th and 18th centuries dealt with the worth of property and human labor. John Locke had argued that things acquire value through labor. Adam Smith argued that this labor should be guided by the invisible hand of capitalism. A society that let its people prosper through their unencumbered industry would be the best of all societies:

"By directing [his] industry in such as manner as its produce may be of the greatest value, he intends only his own gain, and he is in this, as in many other cases, led by an invisible hand to promote an end which was not part of his intention. Nor is it always the worse for the society that it was no part of it. By pursuing his own interest he frequently promotes that of the society more effectively than when he really intends to promote it."
—The Wealth of Nations, 1776

Adam Smith

Writing the Constitution

These ideas about the nature and rights of man and the importance of commerce were modern ideas, self-consciously so. They formed the background for one of America's most important political documents: **the Constitution** (1787). "We the People of the United States, in Order to form a more perfect Union, establish Justice, insure domestic Tranquility, provide for the common defense, promote the general Welfare, and secure the Blessings of Liberty to ourselves and our Posterity, do ordain and establish this Constitution for the United States of America."

Thus begins a very formal and dry sounding set of rules for the governing of these United States.* What's important is that these rules establish a representative democracy and the procedures that ensure the legitimacy of governmental actions.

> "Section. 1. All legislative Powers herein granted shall be vested in a Congress of the United States, which shall consist of a Senate and House of Representatives.
>
> Section. 2. The House of Representatives shall be composed of Members chosen every second Year by the People of the several States..."

In 1791, and with some debate over whether it was necessary, a **Bill of Rights** was added through a series of amendments (First Amendment: "Congress shall make no law respecting an establishment of religion, or prohibiting the free exercise thereof; or abridging the freedom of speech, or of the press...").

---

* Montesquieu, whose *Spirit of the Laws* influenced the writing of our constitution, claimed that the structure of government, not some appeal to first principles, is the best defense of liberty.

The Federalist Papers

JOHN JAY

JAMES MADISON

ALEXANDER HAMILTON

After the Constitution was drawn up, it needed to be ratified so as to express the will of the people. But a number of articles and letters soon appeared that cautioned against adopting a constitution that placed power in a Federal Government. To counter these Anti-Federalist attacks and to explain and justify the new constitution, James Madison, Alexander Hamilton, and, to a lesser degree, John Jay wrote a series of articles for New York newspapers that became known as the Federalist Papers. Taken together, they represent an important contribution to American political philosophy.

The authors argue for a republican form of *representative democracy* ("republic" means absence of monarchy). In some of the most famous articles, Madison was able to address earlier concerns about the possibility of democracy by emphasizing the passions of our differences, the continental size of America, and the separation of powers:

> *"By a faction, I understand a number of citizens, whether amounting to a majority or a minority of the whole, who are united and actuated by some common impulse of passion, or of interest, adversed to the rights of other citizens, or to the permanent and aggregate interests of the community. There are two methods of curing the mischiefs of faction: the one, by removing its causes; the other, by controlling its effects."* (No. 10)

We can't and shouldn't do the former (e.g., make everyone conform); but we can control the effects of this natural condition and even use it to our government's advantage. First, we need to see that democracies work best when they cover vast territories. Here the natural interests of individuals will be spread across different regions (north and south) and different locations (towns and country). Into this mix enter personal associations (religions and sports) and areas of employment (farming and milling). It will be hard to have majorities that compose single-minded affiliations.

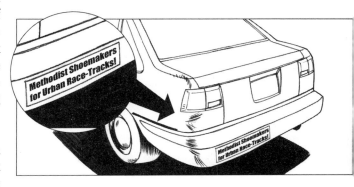

Now we need a form of government that places even these watered down factions in creative opposition to each other. We do this through a *separation of powers*—legislative, executive, and judicial—each of which will have their own interests to follow.

- We further separate the Congress (the legislative branch) into a House of Representatives (closer to the people) and a Senate (more prone to deliberate).
- The judiciary will have an independent Supreme Court. And, since both the legislature and the constitution (which we are now ratifying) depend upon the will of the people, the courts may legitimately be used to control the legislature in matters concerning the constitution. This could be a safety valve preventing the tyranny of the majority over the rights of the minority.

- *"This independence of the judges is equally requisite to guard the Constitution and the rights of individuals from the effects of those ill humors, which the arts of designing men, or the influence of particular conjunctures, sometimes disseminate among the people themselves, and which, though they speedily give place to better information, and more deliberate reflection, have a tendency, in the meantime, to occasion dangerous innovations in the government, and serious oppressions of the minor party in the community." (No. 78)*

This is a very modern view of democracy. It uses a political science that recognizes human nature and it controls the worst of this nature through a system of government based upon checks and balances (the mechanics of ambition checking ambition). It tries to describe how private, self-interested "economic men" could maintain democratic institutions.

Original Intent?

Speaking of modern, a very contemporary debate concerning the constitution and the role of the courts has recently ignited over the role of the courts to determine social-value issues like abortion, same-sex marriage, and end-of-life decisions. There are those who say that the Constitution is a living document and that the courts have a role in using its basic principles to address, judiciously, new circumstances. Others say that it is a bounded document whose statements are literally restricted and cannot be adjusted according to the times.

WILLIAM BRENNAN

Supreme Court Justice William Brennan argued that "the precise rules by which we have protected fundamental human dignity have been transformed over time in response to both transformations of social conditions and evolution of our concepts of human dignity" (lecture at Georgetown University, 1985). While holding on to the "overarching principles" of the Constitution, it is possible to articulate principles implicit in the intent of the basic law that can serve us in our contemporary setting (like the right to privacy).

WILLIAM REHNQUIST

Chief Justice William Rehnquist disagreed. His disagreement, however, did not imply that social values issues were off bounds, only that they needed to be addressed by the legislative process, not the judicial one.

35

> *"The brief writer's version of the living Constitution, in the last analysis, is a formula for an end run around popular government. To the extent that it makes possible an individual's persuading one or more appointed federal judges to impose on other individuals a rule of conduct that the popularly elected branches of government would not have enacted and the voters have not and would not have embodied in the Constitution, the brief writer's version of the living Constitution is genuinely corrosive of the fundamental values of our democratic society."*
> —*The Notion of a Living Constitution* (1976).

Take this with a grain of salt. Before Roe *v.* Wade, different states had different laws with regard to abortion rights. Imagine all 50 states engaged annually in social-value debates over these issues. On the other hand, maybe this is what it means for the democratic process to be "hard"—and maybe over time the debates may wane as well as wax (as they might over same-sex marriage).

At any rate, this is about as close as you can get today to the kinds of "constitutional discussions" that our Founding Fathers had....

Themes of the Ancients and the Moderns

Returning to the earlier debate: What the arguments of the Federalist Papers seem to leave out is the soul of earlier models of democracy—the virtues of its citizens and the pursuit of the common good over individual interests. These were some of the themes of the ancients—the writers of the Federalist Papers were aware of this and so was Thomas Jefferson along with some of the Anti-Federalists.

Many framers of the Constitution were committed to the idea that government should be run by men of virtue whose guiding principles would be the Common Good of all. In the beginning, we didn't elect our state senators, they were selected (supposedly for their talent and virtue).

Some thought that the modern ideas of self-interest and checks and balances would lead men to act selfishly and make the political process too adversarial. Indeed, this happened—parties aligned with different fractions (interest groups) soon appeared. President Washington's farewell address (1796) spoke sadly of this "alternate domination of one fraction over another" and how "in governments purely elective, [the] spirit [of party] is not to be encouraged," opting instead for a country governed according to "consistent and wholesome plans, digested by common counsels and modified mutual interests."

Party Politics

But the cat was out of the bag. Some felt that the Federalists had aligned themselves too closely with a strong central power and they began to call themselves "Republicans."

And the presses jumped in—attacking Federalists and Republicans alike. The cartoon above shows Republican Mathew Lyon and Federalist Robert Griswold fighting on the floor of Congress.

Things got so bad that, under President Adams (who followed Washington), a Sedition Act (1798) was passed, holding newspapers accountable for "false, scandalous and malicious" attacks against Congress or the President.

By the way, the Republican Party as we know it today arose in the 1850s and aligned itself with the anti-slavery movement. Its first elected president was Abraham Lincoln. One of the founders of the Republican Party, Alan Bovay, called it the Republican Party in part to link it to Thomas Jefferson, who had earlier chosen "Republican" to refer to his party.

Themes from the British Utilitarians

This tension between modern views and ancient values was addressed from another angle in the legislative writings of the 19th century British utilitarians. Seeking to overcome the debates and subtleties of many moral philosophers, the utilitarians placed an emphasis on weighing the consequences of an action or policy on the amount of pleasures or pains brought about by those consequences. This formed the basis of the Principle of Utility which noted that those actions or policies that brought about more good (pleasure/happiness) or less evil (pain/unhappiness) are to be approved on a somewhat objective basis.

Jeremy Bentham (1748-1832) applied this principle more broadly to democratic theory.

For Bentham, the institution of democracy provides a balance between the public and its politicians by forcing the self-love of the legislator to heed the interests of his constituency. In this, Bentham was following an earlier writer, Beccaria: "the legislator...erects his edifice on the foundation of self-love, and contrives, that the interests of the public shall be the interest of each individual." All very modern, this.

Here are some quotes from Bentham's reflection on democracy: "To render the conduct of *rulers* conducive to the maximization of happiness, it is not less necessary to employ, in their case, the instrument of *coercion* that in the case of the *rulees*..." (*Constitutional Code*). To insure that such coercion occurs, "two words, viz. *democratical ascendancy*, will, in principle, suffice..." (*Plan for Parliamentary Reform*).

39

What does this mean? It means that, say, a person on City Council needs to ensure that he or she is attending to the needs of the constituents. If he or she doesn't meet these needs, forget about getting elected again. This, in turn, will certainly dash any chances of running for Mayor (the 'democratical ascendancy' that all politicians seek).

And how can it be that the people (the constituents) know what is best? Well, as Benthan famously said:

> *"It is not every man that can make a shoe; but when a shoe is made everyman may tell whether it fits him without difficulty. Every man cannot be a shoemaker but any man may choose his own shoemaker."*

If the trash is suddenly picked up every two weeks instead of every week, you can smell the difference. You don't have to be an expert in public works to know that something is wrong with this policy.

Bentham saw how this state of affairs could be conveyed to the councilman:

> *"The Public Opinion Tribunal is to the Supreme Constitutive what the judiciary is to the Supreme Legislative.... Public Opinion may be considered as a system of law, emanating from the body of the people.... To the pernicious exercise of the power of government it is the only check; to the beneficial, an indispensable supplement."*
> —Constitutional Code

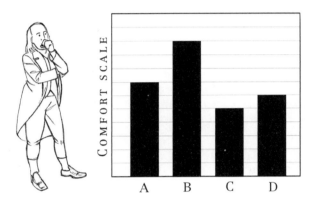

So here we once again see how a modern idea of democracy functions. And we have a glimpse of the role that modern pubic opinion might play in the democratic process.

John Stuart Mill (1806-1873) was a utilitarian like Bentham. But he expanded the notion of "happiness" to include those more subtle pleasures in life like the enjoyment of reading and listening to music (which are hard to quantify in terms of pluses and minuses—+1.4 for Bach, -2.7 for Bon Jovi?).

Like Bentham, he was concerned with improving society and is famous for his support of women's rights.

JOHN STUART MILL

41

In *On Liberty* (1859), he fought rigorously against restrictions of expression (in speech or action)—such censorship and censoring is counterproductive. It's no longer just the tyranny of kings that one needed to watch out for, but the crowd itself—in its attitudes toward woman, homosexuality, different religions, and different peoples.

> *"Society can and does execute its own mandates: and if it issues wrong mandates instead of right, or any mandates at all in things with which it ought not to meddle, it practices a social tyranny more formidable than many kinds of political oppression, since, though not usually upheld by such extreme penalties, it leaves fewer means of escape, penetrating much more deeply into the details of life, and enslaving the soul itself. Protection, therefore, against the tyranny of the magistrate is not enough; there needs protection also against the tyranny of the prevailing opinion and feeling; against the tendency of society to impose, by other means than civil penalties, its own ideas and practices as rules of conduct on those who dissent from them...."*

As long as the thoughts and actions of an individual (e.g., a lesbian who writes books about being a lesbian or a Muslim who criticizes the Koran) do not directly harm others, society should exercise self-restraint. Democracies should tolerate life-experiments. Individuals can grow through this process (even changing their minds) and others can come to understand—or argue with more awareness against—these choices and words.

Mill's position has—along with Locke's and the arguments of the Federalist Papers—become part of the expanding sphere of civil liberty.

Such freedom, Mill believed, encourages individuality and is an indispensable ingredient for human flourishing and social progress.

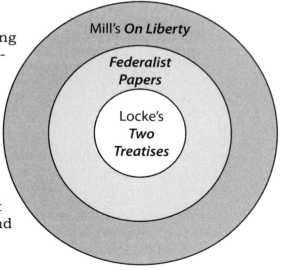

Mill's *On Liberty*

Federalist Papers

Locke's *Two Treatises*

Expanding Sphere of Civil Liberties

But for others, this freedom is a license to infest culture with corrupting ideas and beliefs (mostly dealing with sex and unusual behavior and strange ideas). This counts as a real threat in the minds of many and serves as a source of our culture wars, both nationally and globally.

In the 1830s a Frenchman, **Alexis de Tocqueville** (1805-1859), traveled to America to observe this new democracy and to compare it to the Europe he knew. He published his observations under the title *Democracy in America.*

ALEXIS DE TOCQUEVILLE

"Among the novel objects that attracted my attention during my stay in the United States, nothing struck me more forcibly than the general equality of condition among the people. I readily discovered the prodigious influence that this primary fact exercises on the whole course of society; it gives a peculiar direction to public opinion and a peculiar tenor to the laws; it imparts new maxims to the governing authorities and peculiar habits to the governed.

"I soon perceived that the influence of this fact extends far beyond the political character and the laws of the country, and that it has no less effect on civil society than on the government; it creates opinions, gives birth to new sentiments, founds novel customs, and modifies whatever it does not produce. The more I advanced in the study of American society, the more I perceived that this equality of condition is the fundamental fact from which all others seem to be derived and the central point at which all my observations constantly terminated."

But de Tocqueville also anticipated the problem of "atomism," of free and equal citizens isolated and socially weak. To address this, he noted the importance that Americans placed on all kinds of associations (Moose Lodges, bands, Knights of Columbus, charities, etc.). And he praised local autonomy such as could be found in the New England town meeting (which seemed to combine elements of ancient citizenship and modern individuality).

In the late 1800s another visitor to the United States, **James Bryce** (1838-1922), sought to update de Tocqueville's observations in a series of volumes called *The American Commonwealth* (1888).

By now American politics had settled into more or less a two party system and this formed the basis for much activity at the local, state, and national levels. Bryce shrewdly noticed the growing role of public opinion taking hold in the United States (not unlike what Bentham had imagined):

JAMES BRYCE

44

At times critical, at times supportive, Bryce's work was admired by both Teddy Roosevelt and Woodrow Wilson.

Born the same year de Tocqueville died, **John Dewey** (1859-1952) became known for his contributions to a philosophy of democracy, one based upon American Pragmatism. For pragmatists like Dewey, emerging social conditions require creative (useful/workable) responses.

John Dewey

Society is seen as dynamic, with new and novel problems constantly emerging.

"Conflict is the gadfly of thought" and the "method of democracy—insofar as it is that of organized intelligence—is to bring these conflicts out into the open where their special claims can be seen and appraised, where they can be discussed and judged in light of more inclusive interests than are represented by either of them separately."   —from *Human Nature and Conduct* and *Liberalism and Social Action*

To assist in these appraisals, he suggests a "method of intelligence" that observes facts, constructs hypotheses, and tests consequences. But this method must also connect to a social intelligence that weighs in and responds to policies that may be implemented. This indirect consequences test would check potential state abuses through the public's presence in a representative democracy

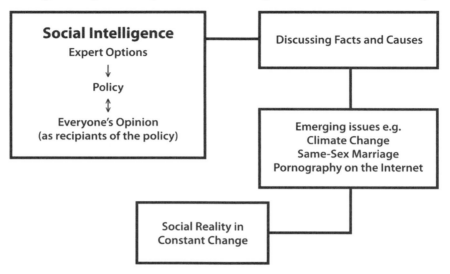

Example: Debates over whether we have a right to die started years ago with advances in medical technology. Patients who would have died naturally from their awful injuries or deadly diseases in times past now faced the prospect of not only being saved (which is a good thing) but also of having their death drawn out. In those cases, a patient in the terminal stages of cancer, for instance, may ask his physician to withhold these extraordinary means of medical technology. As a society, we are still trying to figure out what to do.

Dewey suggests that we gather as much information as we can. We contrast and compare expert opinions and, eventually, we formulate policy. But we have to keep an eye on the consequences of the policies we come up with—we have to see how the public reacts and adjust our policies in light of further experience, evidence, and discussion.

Dewey passionately believed that education needed to play a key role in American Democracy, just as Thomas Jefferson said. This public should be educated in the ways of democracy through a public school system designed to produce students whose natures have been democratized.

The point is, democracy is not just a form of government, but a way of life.

A Rational Foundation for Democracy

While Dewey was recognized for being America's philosopher of democracy, an entirely different take on democracy was emerging from the field of political science. Work done by early rational choice theorists looked at the competition between Democracy, Fascism, and Communism and sought to provide a new rationale for democracy.

Imagine yourself in a position to choose the best form of government. What kind of procedure could we find that would help us do this in an unbiased way?

John Rawls (1921—2002) proposes a thought-experiment: Imagine that you are in an Original Position whereby (a) you actually don't know anything about yourself in particular—what gender or race your are, whether you are healthy or ill, rich or poor, privileged or marginal— but (b) you do somehow know a great deal about how markets work, how people behave and think, i.e., you know a great deal about how society works.

John Rawls

You also understand that societies will always involve social and natural inequalities (some are born on the wrong side of the tracks while others are born with silver spoons in their mouths; some are less able—physically and/or mentally—than others). So it goes. This is life.

Now, given the situation you are in (Rawls says you are behind a Veil of Ignorance), choose the kind of political institution you would wish to find yourself "born into." Oh, one other thing: suppose that someone controls the "lottery of life" and places you in the least well-off position in that society. You now must adopt a strategy that would give you the best possible chance at life given the minimal circumstances that you find yourself in (this is called a Maximin Strategy).

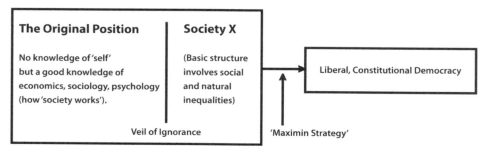

Given this setting, you wouldn't want to choose a feudal society (because you would be a serf, never able to rise about your condition); you won't want to choose a theocracy (because you would be in the heretical minority or someone in the lower caste). The more you think about this, the clearer it becomes that the rational choice is a democracy with a liberal constitution—a political institution that guarantees fundamental rights and the opportunity to exercise those rights through elections, town hall meetings, etc.

Democracy at least gives you a chance.

The Concepts and Problems of Democracy

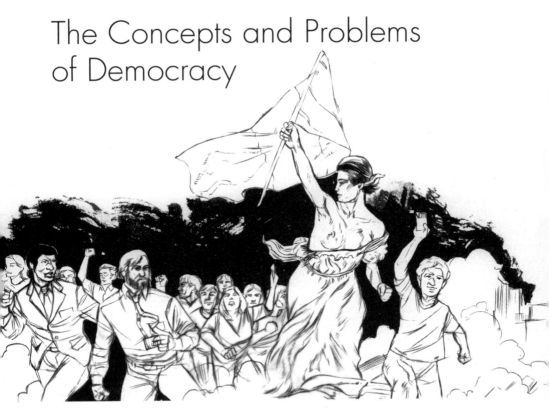

Throughout history, we've seen the emergence of liberty and equality as fundamental human values now universally recognized. And we've seen how democratic constitutions seem to embed these values (e.g., as giving people the freedom to vote and counting the vote of each as equal).

We've seen how modern notions of man influenced the design of the American constitution (separating powers and allowing fractions working against fractions in order to introduce moderation through checks and balances). We've also seen how the workings of democracy can be formalized through procedures guaranteed by its constitutions.

And we've seen how a mechanized constitution can be nurtured by the ancients' sense of citizenship and how the varied aspects of civic virtue could be cultivated at the local level and through education (Jefferson, Tocqueville, Dewey).

But the history of democracy can only take us so far.

49

Now it's time to look directly at the concept of democracy itself. We know that it is a "rule of the many" but we also know this notion has strong critics. How can we justify our belief in democracy? Rawls gave us one way to look at this.

Another way to look at this is to ask whether *democracy is something good itself* (we simply know it is good like we know the color yellow when we see it) or whether *democracy is good because of other goods* that we can describe in more detail (like the moral values of liberty and equality).

Here's a diagram to help us through this maze:

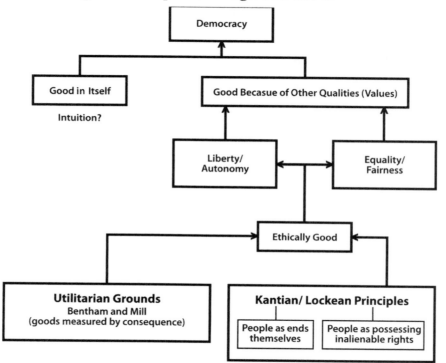

Imagine trying to defend the institution of democracy to someone from another culture where people are ruled by dictatorship or an aristocracy or a theocracy. They won't be impressed by appeals to an intuition—

"Can't you see that it's the best form of government?"   "Umm, no."

They might just not share your perception. So it's best to try to justify democracy by providing an argument.

Here the argument goes like this: Democracy is a good—even the best—form of government because it rests on and supports the fundamental human values of liberty and equality. Those other forms of governance are hierarchical—not everyone has basic liberties or they are not treated as equals (think of the British class system with its nobles and lords or a theocracy in which women are prevented from driving or voting).

Now liberty and equality are not just fundamental values, they are moral values and can themselves be justified on moral grounds.

In general, there are two approaches one can take: a utilitarian perspective or a rights-based perspective.

1. *Utilitarians* could argue that the values of liberty and equality are justified by the effects they have on society and individuals. Within democratic institutions, we get the best results by allowing people the freedom to express their views (remember Mill's *On Liberty*) and individuals feel empowered and taken seriously.
2. *Rights-based* approaches argue for the intrinsic dignity of all human beings and say that bears directly on respecting people's autonomy and basic equality.

We don't have to look at the justifications of these justifications—that would lead us to more fundamental differences concerning which approach is ultimately the right one. And that would soon lead us to what Rawls later called "comprehensive worldviews."

The thicker, more detailed the descriptions of our positions, the less likely it is that we will agree. But not to worry, we need not actually find ultimate answers here—in real world decisions, for instance, these two approaches often play off one another.

Democracy As A Decision Procedure

One important reason that we want democratic institutions is that democracy helps us answer the question: "What ought we to do?" From this perspective, democracy is a kind of decision procedure. Is it a good one? How does it work?

First off, a reality check:

Aristotle reminds us that "it is the mark of an educated man to look for precision in each class of things just so far as the nature of the subject admits" (and this applied to politics as well as ethics).

And Winston Churchill famously said,

"Many forms of government have been tried and will be tried in this world of sin and woe. No one pretends that democracy is perfect or all-wise. Indeed, it has been said that democracy is the worst form of government except all those other forms that have been tried from time to time."

We shouldn't expect our justifications of democracy to be like proofs in geometry; and not everyone will agree with our particular arguments. To look for a knock-out answer in this way is to let the "Perfect become the enemy of the Good."

We should be satisfied with answers that help us understand the concepts and problems and that enable us to defend our positions when we discuss them with others.

And if this book helps *you* get started on this road, then we've done *our* job!

Going back to rights and utilities, we see that each can interpret the other. Rights can be seen as useful—it's good to have them, they bring about happiness; and some goods can be seen as rights ("liberty" is a good that could well be seen as a right).

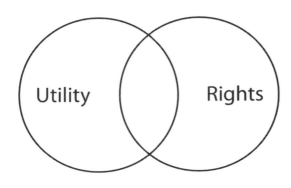

On the formal level, these can be seen as frameworks and both can be kept in play.

At the material level, we often need to decide whether this particular case should be treated more like a utility or more like a right.

Example: What to do about a local airport? Should we expand it or keep it the same?

City officials believe that a small airport near a major university town needs expansion. Such expansion would make it easier for researchers and business people to fly in and out of the town more efficiently and often in a single day. Such research and commercial activity will bring more resources into the area and potentially increase the tax base. But to lengthen the field, a number of houses would have to be vacated and destroyed. What should the town do?

A dictator might simply throw the people out and take a kickback as well. But how should a democracy proceed?

Here's a case where the overall utility might outweigh the rights of the few individuals affected. This can be tricky. It's a classic case of eminent domain since the airport serves a common good.

Now no government can exist where individuals have "absolute vetoes" (I don't want to pay my taxes, buckle my seatbelt, walk down the street with my clothes on).

But just because you don't have an absolute veto, it doesn't mean you won't have a voice (and a vote). In a democracy we expect that government policy and action must be justified and open to comment and debate. Perhaps because of this, any decision regarding the expansion of the airport would be aired in public hearings. The positions put forth would have to include details about fair compensation to those affected by the decision and even proposals to make the area affected better off than it was before the expansion (added attention to the ecology of the area).

In these hearings we'd get the arguments for and against and the voices of those affected. People would also take note of this process and its fairness and remember if things went well or poorly next time there's an election for mayor or city council (recall Bentham's "democratical ascendancy").

In the real world it's much messier than this, of course. But we are discussing concepts. And here it's important to note that there are often going to be trade-offs between what we as a society (city, state, nation) need and what we as individuals want. These include such basic things like clean water, public transportation, nice parks, working sewers, a strong military. You get the point. At the conceptual level, it's a discussion of utilities and rights.

Now let's look more closely at the moral values that relate to the concept of democracy. For if democracy promotes these values, then they become its foundation. That is, we value democracy because it promotes liberty and equality.

— The Value of Liberty —

You know what liberty is when you don't have it. If a government tries to prohibit the gathering of three or more people in public places, we'd say this violates our constitutional right to "free assembly" (to gather, to discuss issues, to protest).

Liberty can be seen as a political dimension of freedom, one of our most cherished values. It is that freedom to pursue your goals and develop your talents. It is what attracted the huddled masses to America, "yearning to be free."

The concept of liberty is also related to the concept of autonomy and autonomy implies self-rule (at the individual and political level).

But here's a problem: Is self-rule really compatible with democracy (e.g., rule by majority decision)? How can we have both individuals with rights and government with power?

There's a tradition, of course, that deals with this and it's the Contract Theory (remember Hobbes and Locke?). By entering into civil society we "freely choose" to place limits on our right to have absolute vetoes on social decisions affecting us.

Take the example of voting. When you cast your vote in an election, you may hope that your candidate wins, but you need to be prepared to accept a different outcome.

There will always be another day and another election. As members of a democratic society, we don't pick up arms and fight when we lose an election or when we disagree with a government policy.

So we accept limits on our liberties. But we expect good reasons for these limits and fair procedures for determining those limits. That's part of our contract.

— The Value of Equality —

While clearly not everyone is equal in size and health and talents, the value of equality comes in at the level of equality under the law and, more deeply, at the level of moral equality.

Like liberty, you know what equality is when you don't have it. When blacks and women were excluded from voting, the arguments were that they were not equal to white males in some sense. That "some sense" (they were labeled as either part property or too emotional) eventually proved unacceptable in a government whose constitution declared that "all men are created equal."

No one in a democracy can claim a special status because of his birth (as the nobles of old did) or gender or race. As Bentham said, "everybody to count for one, nobody for more than one."

Of course, when you have majorities that outweigh minorities, the minority opinions are not treated equally; they lose. But here it's important to distinguish equal procedures from equal outcomes:

- *Input*, for example, via voting, is *treated equally* (each counts as one)
- *Output* is *not equal* (e.g., the airport will be expanded)

In terms of these inputs and outputs, Ross Harrison, author of *Democracy*, says: "This output is the inevitable consequence of a system which has equality enshrined in its input. The input, the democratic procedure, is the core of the system."

The concept of equality at this position gives democracy one of its central moral foundations.

Ross
Harrison

There's a deeper level of equality characterized by John Rawls in terms of two moral powers.

As citizens, we each have a sense of fairness that allows us to get into another person's shoes and see the world as they experience it. In conversations with others, we are able to listen to them and their positions as they are able to listen to us. We have a sense of fairness and reciprocity. This is a kind of moral power that we all have as human beings; it's lacking in cats and clams.

We also have a capacity for a conception of the good. We have our values and our beliefs—not dictated directly by the government, but cultivated and developed through our upbringing and all the people, books, and experiences we've encountered in our life. This value horizon constitutes our "strong preferences" as Charles Taylor has said. It's what gives our life meaning.

It's this deeper level of equality that we experience in open and free discussions with others. And, as we'll see, a "deliberative democracy" makes much of these concepts.

Social Choice Critiques of Democracy

In the light of fascism and communism as competing models of society in the 20th century, some intellectuals in the 1940s and 50s sought to ground the justification for democracy on rational choice instead of moral values like liberty and equality.

The phrase "rational choice" is a highly technical notion of human reason that assumes an axiom of self-interest and a model of calculation based on utilitarian principles. Today the field of Rational Choice is immense and not everyone agrees with this early definition. But the impulse for using rational choice in a justification of democracy can be seen by recalling John Rawls's argument: Given that you won't know who you are and where your place in society would be, it would be rational for you to choose the political institution that would give you a fair go at it even if you found yourself in the most disadvantaged of positions.

So far, so good. But a number of economists and political scientists, many of whom studied at the think tank RAND during the middle of last Century, began to notice logical problems and paradoxes when you move from individual choices to group or social choices—the basic practical question of political philosophy: "What ought we to do?"

First off, in a democracy, we often settle this question by taking a vote. Kenneth Arrow showed that for choices of three or more, paradoxes immediately arise when calculating individual preferences. Suppose there are three candidates in a presidential race. Imagine each representing a Red, Blue, and Green Party. The Green Party has the least amount of support and many members of that party would rank Blue above Red. But, because most of them vote for the Green Party, they wind up actually allowing the Red Party to win. By voting for the first choice, they actually get their last choice.

Kenneth Arrow

59

William Riker, in *Liberalism Against Populism* (1982), argued that populist parties seeking to try to improve our lot through government programs will invariably trample on our freedoms (in the name of the Will of the People); small governments adhering to classic liberalism are to be desired since the invisible hand of the Market will ultimately produce the best overall results. The (democratic) will of the people is useful in the latter case only to guard against tyrants.

William Riker

To drive home his point, Riker criticized traditional notions of democratic decision-making, i.e., social choices. He drew upon studies showing how these kinds of choices can be influenced by agenda setting and manipulation—he who sets the agenda can frame the topics and order them in ways that will lead to a desired outcome; voters can act strategically by, for example, voting as Independents for the candidate in the opposition party that they think is easiest to beat and then switch to their affiliated party in the general election, seeking to defeat the candidate they voted for in the primary. And on and on it goes.

Michael Cain

The irony is that, by starting out to defend democracy, many social scientists in this tradition became like Riker and his Rochester School—they became skeptical of democracy. As Michael Cain wrote in 2001:

> *"Social choice research shows that policy agreement in a democracy may simply be the product of agenda setting.... This has certainly raised fears among many about the legitimacy of laws in a democracy"*
> —Gerry Mackie in *Democracy Defended*

We'll come back to these "irrationalists" (as Gerry Mackie calls them) when we look at the difference between thin and strong democracies.

Political Frameworks:
The Liberty/Equality Equation

Going back to the fundamental values of democracy, we see that they are also one source of what we could call "political divides." Remember how the earlier Federalist and Republican political parties were divided over the power of central government? We still see that divide in debates over states rights.

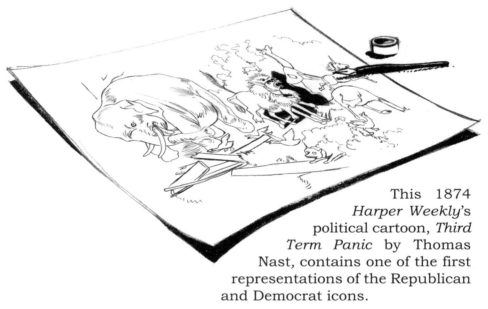

This 1874 *Harper Weekly*'s political cartoon, *Third Term Panic* by Thomas Nast, contains one of the first representations of the Republican and Democrat icons.

Over time parties evolve (and disappear, as with the Whigs and Know-Nothings) and their platforms change (Dixiecrats, Rockefeller Republicans, Social Conservatives).

Today, conservatives emphasize the liberty side of the equation, while progressives emphasize the equality side. Progressives ("liberals") are concerned about inequalities (those who lack health insurance, those who live in poverty) and feel that government can help; conservatives are suspicious of government programs and feel that the market is still be best solution to society's ills.

The truth is probably somewhere in the middle, but this divide brings forth strong emotions—especially in the practice of democracy.

It's the passions of partisanship that are often behind the battles for the hearts and minds and votes of democratic citizens. It gives political campaigns their fire.

They're the source of much of our political debates and the bread and butter of our pundits.

The underlying political frameworks also come in a variety of flavors. Let's look more closely at three: progressives, libertarians and communitarians.

Political Frameworks: The Progressives

"No one deserves his greater natural capacity nor merits a more favorable starting place in society...." —Rawls, 1971

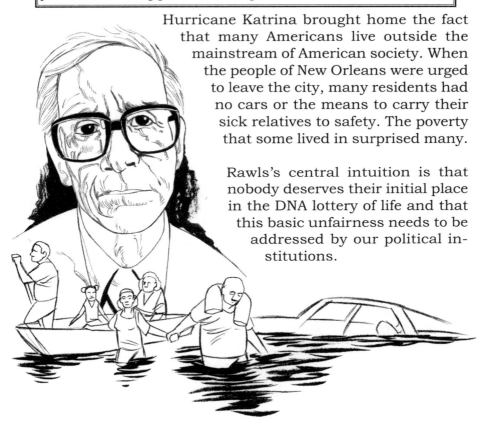

Hurricane Katrina brought home the fact that many Americans live outside the mainstream of American society. When the people of New Orleans were urged to leave the city, many residents had no cars or the means to carry their sick relatives to safety. The poverty that some lived in surprised many.

Rawls's central intuition is that nobody deserves their initial place in the DNA lottery of life and that this basic unfairness needs to be addressed by our political institutions.

Like his argument that of all the political institutions you would want to find yourself part of, you would choose a liberal, constitutional democracy, Rawls also argues that you would want this society to provide you with a fair go at it. For Rawls, this would imply the distribution of primary social goods such as equal opportunities for employment, primary and secondary education, some kind of safety net in times of unemployment or crisis, and so forth. Government programs would assist in this and be funded through a tax scheme in which money from the more well-off would be distributed through government programs to assist the least advantaged. This is part of what he called his "difference principle."

63

Political Frameworks: The Libertarians

The philosopher Robert Nozick blasts Rawls for the injustice of this theory. How so? For Nozick, when we speak of fairness, we mean doing what's fair and it's just not fair to people who have earned their wealth to have the government take that money away from them (through a tax scheme that redistributes that wealth with even the best intentions viz., to help the least well-off). Theft is theft whether it's from a bully or a government Robin Hood.

Robert Nozick

His "Entitlement Theory of Justice" states that whatever is justly acquired can be freely transferred. So if a basketball star earns a million dollars a month, that is his money to use as he wants. He may pay some money to the state for security and basic services, and if he wants to help those in need, he can transfer some of his money to charities or other agencies that help the poor. But the government cannot force him to account for the differences in society. By the way, Ayn Rand's image of man and society fits well with this libertarian perspective.

There's one caveat regarding the original acquisition of this wealth: If the basketball player came by his money by cheating, then he will have to rectify that (that's what the courts will resolve).

But what of the really original holdings?—a stadium in Manhattan sits on a site that was unfairly bargained for in the first place (a few glass beads). Here's where Nozick's theory, at least, starts to become more complex and unworkable (he proposes a radical "reset" for all of society).

Also, there's a key assumption that "all rights boil down to absolute property rights" (and we've seen that this is something that would make government unworkable).

There are more problems with Nozick's model. What about funding for sewers and parks, necessities and amenities that are common goods? And if I am so poor and disadvantaged, all this talk about liberty seems to be a cruel joke. If one were really interested in promoting individual liberties, one should be interested in helping people get a fair go at life—and this takes us back to Rawls. That is, all this emphasis on freedom should entail an interest in creating the basic conditions for people to exercise their freedom—and this should involve some kind of distribution scheme.

At bottom, the difference between Rawls and Nozick (they are both fans of liberal democracies) rests on a fundamental difference in values (the emphasis one places on the values of liberty or equality).

The political philosopher Will Kymlicka looks at it this way:

(1) *Moral Principles* (e.g., Nozick's principle of self-ownership or Rawls's principle of the moral arbitrariness of life's circumstances);

(2) *Rules of Justice* that govern the basic structure of society (e.g., Nozick's three entitlement rules of justice or Rawls's difference principle);

(3) A *particular distribution* of holdings in a given time and place.

A moral principle of self-ownership would make it unjust to tax me in order to help those less well off; but a moral principle that worries about the lot of others might lead me to think that it is just and fair to distribute some of the social goods of society in order to help those who are less well-off.

Will Kymlicka

65

The truth is, we often weigh these values differently in different situations. Sometimes we see the fairness of watching out for others (through, perhaps, requirements to provide Internet access to all schools) and sometimes we recoil from the demands of government regulations (as they may impose unrealistic and unfair practices).

Nozick said later in life that America seems to zig-zag in its political affiliations. Perhaps we do this according to the emphasis we place on these fundamental values. When one value dominates for a while, policies stemming from it tend to become extreme, or rigid, or lead to unintended consequences, and we then move toward the other value.

Political Frameworks: The Communitarians

There is a third framework that sees problems with liberalism itself. It starts with a critique of the liberal belief (either Rawls or Nozick) in self-determination.

Liberals seem to believe that we have the rational ability to step outside our situation and simply determine who we want to be (for Rawls, our material condition may limit our choices, but not our thought about those choices). For communitarians, liberals underestimate the rich tradition of social values under which that capacity can be meaningfully exercised.

We are not atomistic, unencumbered selves—we are situated within a community, embedded in the received wisdom of our human culture. Think of the Amish and of how that society provides a horizon in which life coheres and gets passed down to future generations.

Being an American carries a similar set of values—many of which are derived from the wisdom of our Founding Fathers. For a communitarian, self-awareness is more a matter of interpreting who we already are rather than critically stepping outside of our society and our values.

This has led some social conservatives to adopt a communitarian stand with regard to value issues—questioning the coarseness of our culture with regard to, for example, its sexual mores (promiscuity in popular hip-hop music, pornography on the Internet, etc.).

Communitarian views have also been used to address the loss of connection to our *polis* and the need to reinvigorate our sense of belonging to a community (Putnam's *Bowling Alone*). The neutral state model of liberalism has emphasized negative freedom at the expense of positive freedom.

These large frameworks are not always so neatly separated in our minds—nor in public policy. While liberals like Rawls and Nozick both want to value people's choices, they disagree over the best way to do this. Communitarians remind us that these choices do not occur in a moral vacuum and that they should be guided by the received wisdom of our cultural mores.

THE MORAL COMPASS

Perhaps progressives should be more mindful of the heavy-handedness and bureaucratic demands that can often accompany government policies aimed at addressing inequalities. Perhaps libertarians should appreciate the failures of a purely market-driven approach to society's problems. Kymlicka also points out that:

"The debate between right-wing and left-wing parties is not over the principle of protecting the vulnerable—that is not disputed by either side—but over empirical questions about who really is involuntarily disadvantaged, and about whether redistributive policies actually help them overcome these disadvantages."

And the communitarians might agree that while cultural values are important in shaping us, we can still stand outside of them and judge them from an critical point of view (as liberals urge us to do).

Understanding all this should help us see how democracy is not guided by the search for the One True Opinion, but rather democracy provides a set of procedures for allowing us to muddle through, as best we can, the challenges that face us in an ever-changing world.

Fact of Pluralism

When John Rawls published *Political Liberalism* (1995), he modified certain earlier claims about how to address the social differences one finds in society. His views need not be the only ones. He came to see that modern democracies are characterized by what he called the "fact of pluralism." Not to be confused with relativism (anything goes and is equally justified), political pluralism is characterized by the following criteria:

• A diversity of comprehensive doctrines is a feature of the public culture of democracy (the fact of pluralism). Political frameworks are but one set of comprehensive doctrines. Moral and religious frameworks, sometimes overlapping with political frameworks, form another part of our visions of the good.

• Only oppressive use of force can maintain the common affirmation of one comprehensive religious, philosophical, or moral doctrine. Suppose that others insist that they hold the One True Opinion and that you must adhere to it. This would run counter to our whole tradition (pilgrims came here to escape that kind of life). But so much of our political discourse today (with the other side seen as the enemy) sounds as if one of these frameworks must be the True One.

• A secure democratic regime must be freely supported by at least a majority of its politically-active citizens. Our constitution guarantees fairness of procedures; its mechanical nature favors no particular political party. It is by the people and for the people—as long as it remains possible for it to live up to its ideas, it should we worthy of the support of the people. Such support is critical for the stability of the regime.

• A democratic, political culture has certain fundamental ideas (e.g., liberty and equality) that make it possible to argue for a political conception of justice. We may disagree over the foundations for our fundamental ideas (some may see these values as Kantian or Utilitarian or Biblical), but we can achieve an overlapping consensus in regard to the constitutional essentials (for example—freedom of assembly, freedom of the press, freedom of speech).

Why is it that we seem to disagree over so many important judgments? Well, the sources of reasonable disagreement arise from:

- Differences in ascertaining evidence, weighing evidence, analyzing hard cases.
- Differences in life experience/value formation and its influence on the interpretation of evidence and cases.
- Basic conflicts of values and disagreements over the ordering of values.

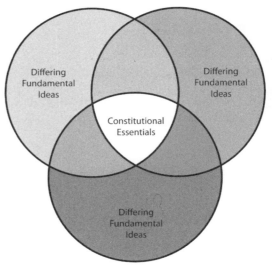

People can look at the same numbers regarding the future of Social Security and come up with different policy solutions. How so? Because they will weigh the evidence differently, some looking for more government involvement and others for a more market-oriented approach. They'll tell different stories about who we are and what we, as a nation, value. There's nothing wrong with such disagreements, they are the outcome of pluralism.

As a democracy, we must work through these problems and perhaps find smart compromises along the way.

Two Models of Democracy: Thin and Strong

Liberal democracies of the kind we see forming around the world are only the beginning of what Benjamin Barber has called "strong democracies." Thin, liberal democracies provide the constitutional essentials of universal suffrage, freedom of press and assembly, etc., but this in no way guarantees that the citizens of these societies will see themselves as any more than isolated individuals who periodically vote (if they choose to do so).

Benjamin Barber

Recent work in citizenship theory makes it clear that, as Kymlicka writes:

"...the health and stability of a modern democracy depends not only on the justice of its basic institutions, but also on the qualities and attitudes of its citizens."

These qualities and attitudes are often highlighted by proponents of Deliberative Democracy and emphasize the role of the citizen in becoming a truly informed and engaged individual, a person willing to listen to all sides and willing to let the force of the better argument (in all its richness) become a guide to opinion formation.

These deliberative practices of democracy are the best response to the critiques of the social choice theorists.

The Market

In 1956 Anthony Downs published *An Economic Theory of Democracy*—a classic work that applies the ideas of the marketplace to the public sphere. For Downs, *homo economicus* becomes *homo politicus*; our rational, self-interested nature engages in manipulation and agenda-setting in order to achieve the highest aggregate (total) of votes.

On this model, our liberal constitution gives us the liberty to vote, but politics becomes a strategic game of getting the most votes in order to win elections, to achieve our preferences.

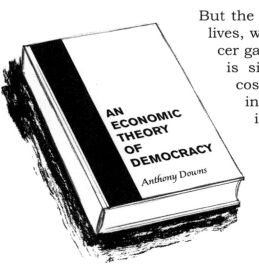

But the irony is that, in our busy lives, with school to go to or soccer games to take the kids to, it is simply not worth it (in a cost/benefit analysis) for the individual citizen to become informed about the issues of the day (e.g., proposed state cuts to Medicaid)—and furthermore, even if they did become informed, the chances that their vote would actually make a difference are statistically nil (or almost so).

This led Downs to his "Citizen-Rationality Hypothesis":

Prop. 12: "Because nearly every citizen realizes his vote is not decisive in each election, the incentive of most citizens to acquire information before voting is very small."

Prop. 13: "A large percentage of citizens—including voters—do not become informed to any significant degree on the issues involved in elections, even if they believe the outcomes to be important."

TWO ECONOMISTS ON ELECTION DAY

But it gets worse: In the *The Myth of the Rational Voter*, Bryan Caplan argues that individual voters are clueless and best advised to remain so. At bottom, they don't know economics and economic policies (like economists do). "Caplan's complaint," wrote a reviewer in the *New York Times Magazine*, "is not that special-interest groups might subvert the will of the people, or that government might ignore the will of the people. He objects to the will of the people itself."

The Forum

Recalling Bentham's notion that you don't have to be a shoe-maker to know if a shoe fits, and Dewey's notion of social intelligence, we have reason to doubt the skeptics of democratic feedback.

But we'll need more than just lever-pulling and final tallies to get good outcomes from our democratic decision-making. That's where the deliberative democrats come in—and where the metaphor of the Forum replaces that of the Market. Here we can look for a more informed voice of the people, one that goes beyond Plato's critique of mere opinion.

Jürgen Habermas

Habermas is a leading figure in the quest for a more deliberative democracy. In *The Structural Transformation of the Public Sphere* he describes the rise of a more forceful meaning of public opinion in the bourgeois societies of the 17th and 18th centuries. Here the appearance of the press and its demands for more freedom—along with the growth of salons and coffee houses*—gave rise to a new public sphere capable of questioning and arguing with the established state and its aristocratic trappings.

"The opinion of the public that put its reason to use was no longer just opinion: It did not arise from mere inclination but from private reflection upon public affairs and from their public discussion."

On the one hand, public opinion could be the source of wisdom and sagacity, and on the other, a source of check and balance. On both counts, it is now perceived to be essential to the proper running of government—a government, moreover, that now has to make its own deliberations public.

---

* Some of the first coffee houses appeared in Venice, and London eventually had almost 3,000 of them—prompting women to protest the effects of too much caffeine on their husbands. Taverns (public houses or "pubs") also played a key role in the awakening of a more deliberative democracy. The City Tavern in Philadelphia hosted the conversations of many Founding Fathers.

Early "Sunshine Laws" were constitutional movements pointing the way toward greater suffrage and freedom of expression. Connecting these constitutional guarantees to social decision-making, a speaker said before the British House of Commons:

> "It is certainly right and prudent to consult the public opinion...if the public opinion did not happen to square with mine; if, after pointing out to them the danger, they did not see it in the same light with me...I should consider it my due to the king...to retire, that they might pursue the plan that they thought better, by a fit instrument, that is by a man who thought with them...." —Fox, 1792

Today, we call that "fit instrument" an election.

For Habermas, "Fox's speeches were made with the public in mind; 'they,' the subjects of public opinion, were no longer treated as people whom, like 'strangers,' one could exclude from deliberations...step by step the absolutism of Parliament had to retreat before their sovereignty...."

Continuing his historical study, Habermas notes that the term "public opinion" implied that "it was formed in public discussion after the public, through education and information, had been put in a position to arrive at a considered opinion."

He later draws from Peel's "Tamworth Manifesto" (1834) concerning the need for political parties to publish their programs (i.e., platforms) and writes that: "Public opinion was formed in the conflict of arguments concerning a substantive issue, not uncritically based on common sense in either naïve or plebiscitarily [referendum] manipulated assent to or vote about persons. Hence [public opinion] needed a defined issue as its object more than it needed prominent persons."

This is deep: True public opinion is arrived at by discussion of the issues, not something that gets manipulated by the media or determined by the personality of the candidates.

"Open and Informed" Conversations

The public needs to turn its attention to the issues and to the arguments that are put forth regarding those issues. For deliberative democrats, it does so through "open and informed" conversations.

"Openness" refers to the ability of all perspectives to be allowed a voice in the discussion and "informed" refers to the need for the discussion to be based upon the best information and arguments available. These broad requirements of practical reason have been adopted by advocates of deliberative democracy with the goal of achieving a strategy for democratic decision-making on a range of practical political issues.

This marks the conversational or deliberative turn in political philosophy. It sees human reason as essentially dialogical (we think best when we think together)…it requires us to offer public reasons for our positions (no secret or sacred knowledge, only reasons that others can have access to).

So, for example, there are six areas that are up for discussion regarding state cuts to Medicaid. These must be looked at with care—and under the constraint that we can't raise taxes. The more detailed the discussions, the less they turn into debates about the larger issues and the more they turn into problems to be solved.

Inviting citizen participation in these discussions lends legitimacy to outcomes (even though not everyone might agree with the outcomes).

All this comes together again in the quest for a more refined public opinion. James Campbell, quoting from Dewey's *Democracy and Education*, writes: The process of living in a democratic community requires a recognition that our political life "is essentially a cooperative undertaking, one which rests upon persuasion, upon ability to convince and be convinced by reason; or, in ordinary language, upon public opinion."

Citizenship Theory

Democracy is much more than a constitution. It requires citizens to uphold it and make it work. But depending on how we view democracy, we get two different interpretations of citizenship—one is "vote-centric" and the other is "talk-centric."

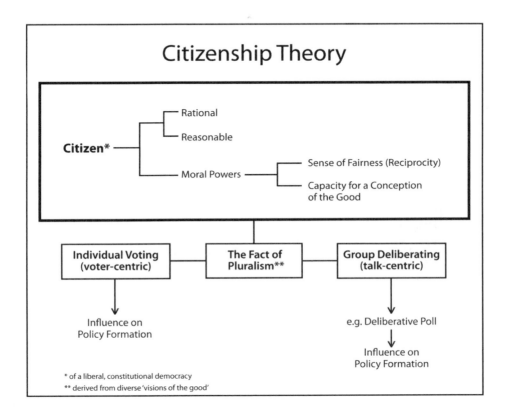

Let's assume that someone is a citizen of a liberal democracy. How should we characterize them? Well, how do you think of yourself?

"You're rational, no doubt": One technical meaning of this term refers to your ability to figure out what you should do if you want something. If you want a cup of coffee, you can figure out that you have to heat water (find a pot, pour water into it, place it on the stove, turn on the gas, etc.). This is called "means/ends thinking"—you know the end (a cup of coffee) and you use your reasoning ability to figure out the means that will get you that coffee. This is also called instrumental reason or calculating reason.

But you're more than just calculating. You are a "reasonable" person. Not everything fits within your calculations. Other people may want to do things you're not interested in—such as ride bikes to work. They may also want the city to help them by creating bike lanes and building bike trails. This may cost you some of your tax dollars. We often accept these losses because, while we disagree with the emphasis those folks place on their biking, we see their position as reasonable and we are willing to go along with it (we might not do this if they wished to erect a statue to the god GORK in our public square because "GORK told them to do it").

IN GORK WE TRUST

We've seen how Rawls characterizes our equality by describing our "moral powers." Our sense of fairness and reciprocity allows us to listen to others and to expect the same from them. Our discussions can rely on arguments and reasons, but also on story-telling and empathy. We expect sincere attempts to craft reasons in terms that we can all understand (even if we disagree).

Now, it's in our capacity for a conception of the good that we often find the sources for our disagreements. Unlike cats or clams, we can form a vision of the good life and this viewpoint varies considerably in modern democratic societies (where we are constitutionally promised "life, liberty, and the pursuit of happiness"—according to our own beliefs). This accounts for the fact of pluralism that we find in modern democracies. It also accounts for the "fractions" that naturally arise out of this pluralism and that form much of the context for our different political frameworks.

Reflective Equilibrium

Our strong preferences are not static. While we often feel a kind of equilibrium regarding our formed opinions, sometimes we encounter situations and perspectives that surprise us and throw us off balance ("I never thought of it that way," we say). This can cause us to alter our beliefs and attitudes somewhat. When this happens, we are widening our reflective equilibrium.

Wide reflective equilibrium represents what we might achieve if our political positions formed not only a consistent, integrated body of beliefs, but also evolved from reflection on many other perspectives and arguments that might affect our positions one way or the other.

This movement toward wide reflective equilibrium requires an openness on our part to discover new facts and listen to new reasons as well as the ability to use our imagination to grasp other perspectives. In this way, wide reflective equilibrium emphasizes the way information can bear on our views. It's a concept that has been discussed much in the literature, but for democratic practice, it boils down to an ability to be open to the on-going challenge of human conversation.

This is an important notion for citizens in a democratic society.

Civic Virtues

We've seen that the Greeks and Romans, and some of our Founding Fathers, placed great emphasis on the attitudes and responsibilities that we take upon ourselves when we act as citizens. Being a citizen is more than just holding a passport that says you are a citizen; It involves the disposition to act like a citizen—to exhibit the *virtues of citizenship.*

What are these civic virtues and can—or should—these be taught?

Traditionally, when you think of yourself as a citizen, you are seeing yourself as part of a community—a political community that values the ideals of liberty and equality, a city and state that has limited resources as well as services and officials, a neighborhood that has home owners, renters, and businesses.

As a citizen, you need to get out of yourself and smell the world around you—and participate in that world...lend a hand, help out, find out about local organizations; read the newspapers, check out local websites, read blogs (not only the ones you agree with).

The first and foremost civic virtue is this disposition to participate in the ongoing activities of your *polis.* This was the very meaning of freedom for the ancients—yet today, many "free" people hardly bother!

William Galston describes four types of civic virtues. The first are general virtues like loyalty and law-abidingness. Violent street gangs, who may be loyal to themselves, certainly don't help their communities and therefore lack these virtues.

 The second are social virtues like independence and open-mindedness. It helps a community when members of the community think for themselves and are open to new ideas and thoughts. Maybe even gang members can cultivate these virtues and alter their behavior.

Economic virtues fit here: cultivating a work-ethic and a responsibility for one's family (paying bills, avoiding debt, making sure the kids delay the self-gratification of watching TV before they do their homework).

Political virtues are the fourth category for Galston: an interest in and ability to discern the rights of others; an interest in and ability to evaluate those in office; and interest in and ability to engage in public discourse.

 To this last point many add the virtue of *toleration*. Because other people may have different ideas about what we ought to do, you need to be able to listen to them (and expect the same from them).

Some have called this the "virtue of public reasonableness"—we can't just demand that others do what we want—or accept our particular faith or set of beliefs as sufficient for agreeing with us. So we need to engage with others in our community with a willingness to listen to all sides, seek solutions to our problems (even if we don't always find them), and commit ourselves to an ongoing interest in our place within our society as a whole.

Countries that only adopt a democratic constitution, without cultivating a sense of citizenship among their people, often fail at achieving a viable society.

How can we help to create a more viable society?

Education is one key factor, not just by reading books, but by creating forums for people to engage in—so that they can actually develop the virtues they read about! Civics classes, English classes, biology classes—all sorts of high school and college curriculum could benefit from exercises that get students to think and work together on issues and problems. We need to cultivate not only "critical thinking," but "deliberative skills."

A word about the virtue of patience:

Some folks who work with community groups occasionally say "democracy would work better without the people." People have real complaints and frustrations, they have different personalities and people skills; they get caught up in rumors and act rude. Sometimes they have had too much coffee. They can be rowdy and the town hall meetings can get disorderly.

Traditional setups for town hall meetings—with the dreaded microphone as the main interface between the public and the government—don't help things much. So care must be taken to structure meetings well: have agendas, time allocations, flexibility, notetakers or moderators of some sort. And put up guidelines that may bring out the best in people ("treat each other with respect," "don't interrupt without asking," etc.).

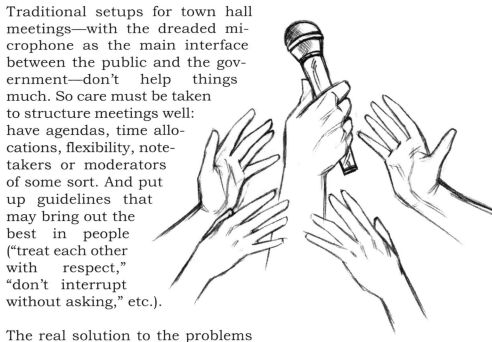

The real solution to the problems of democracy is better democracy!

Strong Democracy and Citizen Forums

Today there are many opportunities to practice deliberative democracy through what could be called Deliberative Loops®. A loop is a feedback mechanism that allows people affected by a policy or policy discussion to participate in the discussion. A loop is deliberative when that discussion is structured through the use of good background materials, moderated conversations, and a survey or final report that reflects the outcomes of the deliberative process.

We see more and more local and regional agencies utilizing forums like "citizen juries," "electronic town hall meetings," "National Issues Forums," and "campus conversations"—all involving two critical aspects of deliberative loops: background information on the issue and a structured environment for discussing the issue.

Surveys of various kinds, often taken before the event as well as afterwards, help to ascertain what the participants thought about these issues after they have discussed them—the results can then be passed on to the policy makers. Thus the conversations can influence decisions.

Participatory strategic planning sessions, used at the community, city, and even state level, can also be seen as forms of deliberative loops.

Here people get together with trained facilitators and brainstorm solutions to problems. Listing interests and then paring down the list to focus on a selected few often leads to new ideas for dealing with

NEW SOLUTIONS

Perspective

problems that the whole group sees as important. It's Dewey's social intelligence and Habermas's dialogical reason at work!

It's not perfect. There are always concerns about the quality and fairness of the background materials and the role that the moderators might play in the discussion. Surveys too can be manipulated. For social choice theorists, these are show-stoppers. But for practitioners of deliberative democracy, they are red flags to be aware of and to be addressed though discussion and protocols. Some questions to consider are:

- Have the materials been developed in a collaborative way, have they been tested in the field?
- Have the moderators been trained to keep the conversation on task and to avoid inserting their own opinions?
- Is everyone abiding by the rules for discussion?
- Are there action plans and practical outcomes built into the process?

It's a second-best world that we live in, we can only try to do our own best within it.

Applying Deliberative Democracy

For the Anti-Federalists, American democracy should be as close to the people as possible. They feared the aristocratic tendencies of a government centered in a capitol far from the everyday concerns of ordinary Pennsylvanians or Virginians.

Madison and the authors of the Federalist Papers argued for a strong central government of representatives (senators) who could deliberate on the common good and avoid the heat of the moment.

In broad outline, the Anti-Federalists emphasized a direct democracy in which each citizen had an equal voice in the activities of their government; the Federalists emphasized a representative democracy in which democratically elected members of Congress (and selected members of the Senate) could deliberate as peers on matters of national importance.

Behind the desire for deliberation was a Madisonian concern with the tyranny of the majority (those greater numbers who vote in their own self-interest). The one side emphasized equality; the other deliberation and fear of majority passions. The more you have equality, the less you have deliberation; the more you have deliberation, the less you have equality.

The dilemma can be broken only if you have an institution that manages to combine majoritarian equality with informed deliberation, and does so, moreover, in a consulting rather than plebiscitary way. Political scientist James Fishkin has given this approach a practical footing through his concept of a Deliberative Poll®.

Deliberative polling is a specific process whereby background information on an issue of local or national importance is developed and presented to a scientific random sample of the population. The sample then gathers in small groups, with a moderator, to discuss and deliberate upon the topic. Questions are invariably generated by the discussions and these questions are given to a panel of experts for response. The groups gather again and then answer a list of survey questions. As Fishkin wrote in *Deliberation and Democracy*, "A deliberative opinion poll models what the electorate would think if, hypothetically, it could be immersed in an intensive deliberative process."

random sample

information

small group discussion

expert panel

small group discussion

survey (poll)

Illustrations by Stacy Innerst. Copyright ©, Pittsburgh Post-Gazette, 2008, all rights reserved. Reprinted with permission.

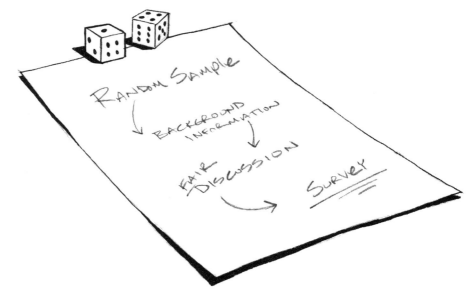

A central element in the protocols for a deliberative poll® is the random sample. As early as the 1930s and 40s, George Gallup showed that you don't need very large numbers of people in order determine the public's views on a matter. A careful mix of age, gender, background, and so forth can actually yield a representative sample of the population. This stratified random sample satisfies the demands of equality.

Caveat: Even if you get a representative sample, give them good information and moderate their conversation, it is still possible to disagree with the results of this kind of poll. The process has a non-tyranny principle bound up with the principles of equality (inclusiveness) and deliberation. It is possible that super-majorities of informed citizens could still get it wrong.

We can distinguish "democratic procedures" (like fair elections) from "democratic values" (like liberty and equality). This allows people to offer principled objections if they disagree with the results. Of course, in the long run, this simply means that the conversation can continue.

Envisioning A Strong Democracy

Carolyn Lukensmeyer thinks big. Her organization, America-Speaks, gathers large crowds—sometimes 1,000 in one room, sometimes 5,000 in coordinated sessions, sometimes 20,000 over a year-long process. Unlike Fishkin's model, which uses random sampling, her group seeks out "convenience samples"—groups from organizations, churches, or anyone interested who sees the announcements. While not as strictly representative as Fishkin's, the large size often reveals a broad spectrum of demographics and viewpoints.

Working with such large groups requires a new kind of town hall meeting. While participants receive background information (about reconstructing New Orleans or fixing California's heath care system) and gather in small groups with trained moderators, they also have access to keypads that electronically convey choices to a central computer for display on a large screen. With such techniques, AmericaSpeaks can create a dynamic "conversation" among thousands of people at the same time.

Suppose the group is asked to pare down six possible approaches to regional planning (resource sharing, taxes, duplication of agencies, duplication of services, and so forth) to the top three that they consider most important and most likely to be acted upon. A screen will display all six options and then, after deliberating, people use their keypads to select the top three that they feel are most likely to be candidates for adjusting. Within minutes, the whole audience can see bar charts displaying the results—which are often quite striking in their clarity. The discussion can then continue, but with some consensus on at least the general weights that citizens might give to the choices confronting them.

Combining Lukensmeyer and Fishkin

Carolyn Lukensmeyer

James Fishkin

Imagine using the techniques of AmericaSpeaks, or other groups like the National Issues Forum, to develop an analysis of and an agenda for proposals to, for example, consolidate regional resources in areas of the country where multiple municipalities overlap with city and county services. There are in fact many areas of the country where municipal divisions go back to 19th century farmlands and where you have 20 or 30 different water authorities.

Start with regional experts and stakeholders hosting meetings where plans and strategies are discussed and initially drawn up. These are more like participatory strategic planning sessions, not white papers or power-point presentations. Reach out to the community to get citizen input and ascertain citizen attitudes and feelings.

Now create an agenda and background materials for larger, structured town hall meetings.

Recruit from civic organizations, churches, flyers in laundro-mats, or announcements in local newspapers. Maybe at these meetings you place maps of the region on the table so that peo-ple can see the areas under discussion and how their fellow tablemates relate to these areas (where to you live and work, what recreational activities and shopping activities take you to different places). All of a sudden, people begin to see them-selves as part of a region, not just their suburb or neighbor-hood. They then begin to think of regional problems and challenges and may come to see that there are a number of im-portant choices to be made.

All the while, stakeholders have been watching and participat-ing and the press has been reporting. Suppose that at the end of the event, data is generated that says that a majority of the participants felt that the region is ripe for change and several action items are highlighted.

As part of the process of gaining citizen support for these changes, take the results and run them though a deliberative poll—if the data here compliments the data from the town hall meeting, you begin to see what the citizens of the region think about these issues (now informed by this citizen participation). You now have real consulting power and a sense of legitimacy is lent to the process—not cooked up in a back room.

Imagine these proposals being refined and then disseminated throughout the community through more forums (including online discussions) and through media exposure.

We then come to the place where the final proposals are hammered out and run through another deliberative poll. If all has gone well and the media has followed this process throughout, you might even be able to run a more traditional poll and discover that the public at large has been paying attention and that this poll, too, supports the proposed changes to the region.

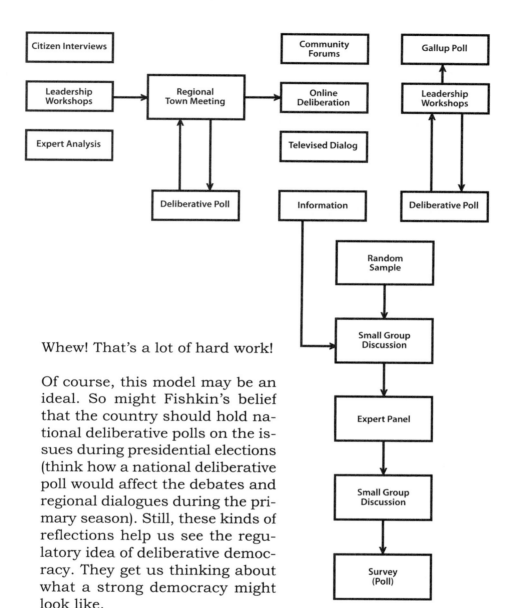

Whew! That's a lot of hard work!

Of course, this model may be an ideal. So might Fishkin's belief that the country should hold national deliberative polls on the issues during presidential elections (think how a national deliberative poll would affect the debates and regional dialogues during the primary season). Still, these kinds of reflections help us see the regulatory idea of deliberative democracy. They get us thinking about what a strong democracy might look like.

Community Conversations: Bringing
Deliberative Democracy to the Neighborhood

Utopias aside, there are many instances of strong democratic practices taking place around the country. Here's one very concrete example:

The Federal Weed and Seed Program helps distressed neighborhoods by providing funds to weed out problems (drugs, gun violence) and seed initiatives to improve safety and quality of life. But applicants to the program have to demonstrate that they are organized and willing to take on the responsibly of working for the betterment of their own community. Ordinarily, this involves creating a steering committee with several subcommittees interested in things like community development and restoration, community policing, and so forth. They meet several times and identify the challenges and opportunities facing them.

In Pittsburgh, we added another dimension to this process by surveying samples of the Hilltop Community (nine different neighborhoods) and inviting them to participate in a day-long community conversation about their community, its challenges, and its opportunities.

> *Interestingly enough, many of the sampled participants identified the same sorts of problems and opportunities— often adding insights and suggestions along the way. The results were put into a proposal submitted by the steering committee to the federal government.*

A little while later, across town, a community organization had been holding talks with a developer about support for their community. But the organization was perceived as not truly representing the community; at a public hearing a group interrupted the meeting and demanded to be heard. It was a typical shouting match as people rushed to the microphone amid calls to order.

This often happens when community members feel that they have not been included in the decision-making, that the process was not transparent and therefore not legitimate. In contrast to all this yelling, the Hilltop Community conversation was full of applause and excitement.

E-Democracy
The Early Days

Ever since the rise of the digital computer in the 1940s, pioneers of the information revolution foresaw the potential of what Joseph Licklider called "man-computer-symbiosis." A daunting phrase, it recognized the interactive relation between computers and human beings. In 1976 Murray Turoff spoke of this relation in terms of communication:

Joseph Licklider

> "I think the ultimate possibility of computerized conferencing is to provide a way for human groups to exercise a 'collective intelligence' capability...in principle, a group, if successful, would exhibit an intelligence higher than any member."

Murray Turoff

During this formative period, another visionary, Douglas Engelbart, saw a time when computers could "augment intelligence" and help human beings in all kinds of ways by "increasing the capability of a man to approach a complex problem situation, to gain comprehension to suit his particular needs, and to derive solutions to problems."

Douglas Englebart

Once computers became connected to one another through inventions like the Ethernet and once this system became linked to networks like ARPANET, the augmentation of intelligence came naturally to be applied to Dewey's social intelligence. As we've seen, for Dewey, this is the kind of intelligence that lies at the heart of democratic endeavors.

In this way, the rise of computer-mediated communications and the link between computers and democracy was underway.

In 1985, a group of hippies and techies set up the "Whole Earth 'Lectronic Link," and began to build a virtual community. Along with other projects, this marked the beginning of cyberspace as well as the beginning of online efforts in democracy.

E-Democracy Takes Hold

More formal efforts of e-democracy soon started as state and federal government agencies began to make information available online and to solicit citizen input through bulletin board forums. After the World Wide Web made these activities feasible for large numbers of people, new initiatives at citizen participation started up. The state of Minnesota took an early lead. And now even neighborhood block watches and graffiti task forces use distribution lists to alert their members about problems, invite them to meetings, and even urge them to appear at hearings where vandals may be sentenced to community service (showing the district judges that the community cares about these issues).

Still, as the blogosphere shows, there's a need for more "e-listening," more deliberative environments. Too often the tone of the web seems crass and self-congratulatory. Reflective work, good work, is there—but it's not usually linked to real dialogue or connected to policy outcomes.

Eventually, online environments informed by the principles of deliberative democracy appeared—UnChat, Web Lab, E-The People. They were all text-based, but they added features like moderators, turn-taking, specific agenda for discussion, and simple voting and survey functions. They provided for structured conversations; they were early examples of "deliberative e-democracy."

Newer tools began to use richer interfaces—and the use of audio and video created a sense of telepresence, allowing people to communicate more naturally. Project PICOLA (Public Informed Citizen Online Assembly) pointed the way and now commercial programs like Adobe Connect and customized products like Vox Populi are beginning to support real online deliberations.

Another example: A group called Soliya uses multimedia Web 2.0 technologies to provide young adults with the skills, knowledge, and relationships they need to develop a nuanced understanding of the issues that confront them. By offering training, tools, and opportunities to convey this understanding to their broader communities, Soliya is empowering young adults to play a constructive role in creating a more informed, just, and peaceful global society—that's the hope, at least.

The mobile Internet is also offering new possibilities. In 2001 thousands of Filipinos gathered at a location called "Edsa" to protest the policies of their president, Joseph Estrada. How did they get there? Text messages went out earlier saying "Go 2EDSA, wear black"—it was a massive use of cellphones to create a political rally, one that eventually brought a change in the presidency.

The Internet and wireless technologies are bubbling and brewing—sooner rather than later we'll be witnessing something like Democracy 2.0—made possible by a new generation of cyber-savvy citizens who will bring the early promises of e-democracy to the whole world!

But be careful, the same pitfalls as well as promises await this version too.

Transnational Democracy

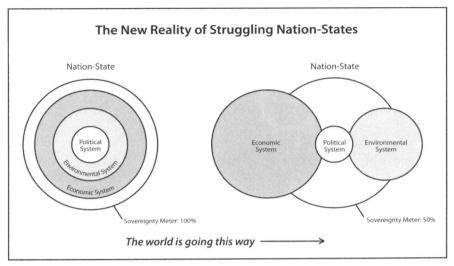

The New Reality of Struggling Nation-States

Nation-State

Political System
Environmental System
Economic System

Sovereignty Meter: 100%

Nation-State

Economic System
Political System
Environmental System

Sovereignty Meter: 50%

The world is going this way ⟶

Today our nation-states are going the way of the old city-states. Our world economy and the impacts of global climate change are making our once sovereign political systems more integrated into a larger world of problems and challenges.

This transition will pose problems for traditional models of democracy since democratic constitutions appear for the most part to be state-bound by political cultures and territorial boundaries. And it is unlikely that we will be willing to create a world government (though we join in intergovernmental agencies, treaties, and collaborations all the time).

But "deliberative democracy should be more at home in the international system" says John Dryzek in *Deliberative Democracy and Beyond*. Transnational civil societies have already created "discursive publics," focusing on areas like energy resources, population growth, global poverty, the environment, etc. So some form of "governance without government" might be possible and, indeed, necessary!

Twenty Global Problems and Twenty Years to Solve Them...

Former World Bank executive, J. F. Rischard, warns that there are growing challenges to world health and security that need to be resolved within the next 20 years whether we want to or not.

For example, international money exchanges and tax schemes will need to be rethought. Many companies now work with teams scattered across multiple borders with little clarity as to how individual countries figure out tax rates; new offshore entities now offer safe havens for companies and individuals alike, cutting into tax revenues for countries that need them; and e-commerce and e-money transactions are outpacing traditional banking and taxing practices developed in the 20th century (with consequences for national security as well as national treasure).

The worldwide financial crisis of 2008 shows how interconnected we all are. It directly affected people's personal finances and demonstrates how important it is for nations and transnational institutions to work together on common problems.

One Example: Climate Change

Scientists have determined that the global climate is warming and that the burning of fossil fuels since the Industrial Revolution has contributed significantly to this warming. Since these fuels (coal and oil) are still used to generate electricity and facilitate transportation, we are confronted with the need to mitigate the effects of these fuels and eventually find substitutes for them.

The Intergovernmental Panel on Climate Change (IPCC) has been looking at this problem for years. It's an example of a transnational governmental agency that is deliberative at its core. It has three groups looking at science (facts) as well as policy (values).

The scientists have concluded that climate change will have significant impacts on—

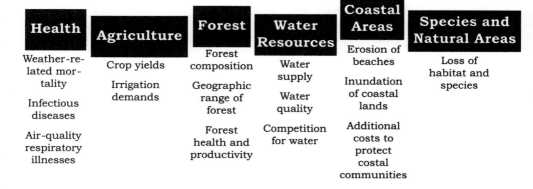

Health	Agriculture	Forest	Water Resources	Coastal Areas	Species and Natural Areas
Weather-related mortality	Crop yields	Forest composition	Water supply	Erosion of beaches	Loss of habitat and species
Infectious diseases	Irrigation demands	Geographic range of forest	Water quality	Inundation of coastal lands	
Air-quality respiratory illnesses		Forest health and productivity	Competition for water	Additional costs to protect costal communities	

We have to make choices here and now; even taking no action is itself a choice. So regardless of where we stand on certain policies, the issue of climate change is making us all more cosmopolitan in our thinking and forcing us to see ourselves as citizens of the world.

As challenging as this problem is, it may mark the beginning of a new era in human history—a time when we come together as a planet to talk about what *we* ought to do.

Conclusion

We *all* have a lot of work to do! But how and where to begin?

Regina Anderson from the Coro Center for Civic Leadership says, "People find it daunting to become involved if they haven't been involved before. They feel it will take a lot of their time. But that's not the case. Think about all of the things you like to do, and how you can blend in your natural tendencies with becoming more involved.

"Think about what your friends are doing. Who do you know that is involved in politics? The beauty of being a young person [Regina is 20-something] is that often, young people are campaign managers, chiefs of staff for city council members. If you don't know people in those roles directly, chances are, you're connected to those people by colleagues, or friends of friends.

"Think about what it is that you want to learn about your city, your state, or the democratic processes that most affects you. To find out more, all you literally have to do is invite the young people involved in your local democracy to lunch to learn more.

"If there's an issue you're passionate about—whether it is local farming, litter, the environment, social injustice, bicycles— there are others around you that are interested in those issues as well. It is amazing how almost any topic can touch your ability to become involved in your community."

If you're older, in your 40s or 50s, you're in a good position to become a mentor to many of the younger members of your community. You're further along your career path, but that means you'll have advice to give and connections to provide. And if you're a retired senior citizen, with the emphasis on *citizen*, you have new kinds of time on your hands—use it to give back to the community.

It's remarkably easy to get involved. Neighborhood groups are always looking for new faces and new ideas. Of course, some groups are not what you have in mind, but there are many others out there. Start your own if you must.

You'll also be surprised at how responsive your councilmen and city and state representatives are—especially if you have something positive to contribute. And if you have problems you want to discuss, bring solutions and not just complaints. That's the best way to get things done.

In many ways, Barack Obama's 2008 presidential campaign developed the best integration of internet and community up to that point. Expanding upon the political party style of that campaign's websites, we can see the groundwork for a more deliberative use of online tools and local, state and national conversations. Communities of discourse can be built around information and organized into forums linked to real outcomes.

This is not only technically possible, but politically important for our democracy—for it's been said that our constitution is less like a blueprint for a house, than a home for a conversation.

So let's get started, and remember:

DEMOCRACY

BEGINS WITH YOU!

Credits

Special thanks to the readers of an early draft, the students and colleagues who worked with me on "Campus Conversations" at Carnegie Mellon, Pittsburgh's Coro Center for Civic Leadership and all those who supported the Southwestern Pennsylvania Program for Deliberative Democracy.

Sources

Here are some of the texts used during the writing of this book. They may be overly academic for beginners, but they influenced the structure and approach of the book. Our book, in turn, can serve as a guide to these works.

Barber, B. R. (1984). <u>Strong democracy : participatory politics for a new age.</u> Berkeley, University of California Press.

Fishkin, J. S. (1995). <u>The voice of the people : public opinion and democracy.</u> New Haven, Yale University Press.

Harrison, R. (1993). <u>Democracy.</u> London ; New York, Routledge.

Kymlicka, W. (2002). <u>Contemporary political philosophy : an introduction.</u> Oxford ; New York, Oxford University Press.

The section on Alfarabi is based on an essay by Muhsin Mahdi in Strauss and Cropsey's *History of Political Philosophy.*

The illustration on nation-state sovereignty is derived from J. F. Rischard's *High Noon: 20 Global Problems/20 Years to Solve Them.*

Resources

Our libraries are one of the most important foundations for democracy. They are keepers of our words and should be one of the first places to go for more information on democracy.

Librarians at your school or in your town's public library can give you personal advice on how to dig deeper into any of the topics described in this book. They can also point you to online resources, including many excellent web-based encyclopedias. Of course, you can get started on your own by doing searches —but be wary of the content you find, since not everything on the web has been well vetted by scholars and researchers.

The mother of all libraries is the Library of Congress. It also has one of the best online sites for exploring our democracy. Here you'll find access many of our most important documents, from the constitution to current legislative initiatives. There are also good resources for teachers and students, from grade school to college. Get started by going to www.loc.gov/

About the Author & Illustrator:

Robert Cavalier received his BA from New York University and a Ph.D. in Philosophy from Duquesne University. In 1987 he joined the staff at Carnegie Mellon's Center for Design of Educational Computing, where he became Executive Director in 1991. Dr. Cavalier was Director of CMU's Center for the Advancement of Applied Ethics and Political Philosophy from 2005-2007. He is currently co-Director of Southwestern Pennsylvania Program for Deliberative Democracy.

Reuben Negrón is a visual artist who works across many fields. He is a regular contributor to the comic book anthology, *Rabid Rabbit*. His work has been published internationally in novels, periodicals and annuals, including *Playboy, Communication Arts* and *Spectrum*. As a fine artist, Reuben's work has been exhibited domestically as well as abroad. He holds a BFA from the Maryland Institute College of Art and an MFA from the School of Visual Arts in New York. He currently lives and works in New York City.

THE FOR BEGINNERS® SERIES

AFRICAN HISTORY FOR BEGINNERS:	ISBN 978-1-934389-18-8
ANARCHISM FOR BEGINNERS:	ISBN 978-1-934389-32-4
ARABS & ISRAEL FOR BEGINNERS:	ISBN 978-1-934389-16-4
ASTRONOMY FOR BEGINNERS:	ISBN 978-1-934389-25-6
BARACK OBAMA FOR BEGINNERS, AN ESSENTIAL GUIDE:	ISBN 978-1-934389-38-6
BLACK HISTORY FOR BEGINNERS:	ISBN 978-1-934389-19-5
THE BLACK HOLOCAUST FOR BEGINNERS:	ISBN 978-1-934389-03-4
BLACK WOMEN FOR BEGINNERS:	ISBN 978-1-934389-20-1
CHOMSKY FOR BEGINNERS:	ISBN 978-1-934389-17-1
DADA & SURREALISM FOR BEGINNERS:	ISBN 978-1-934389-00-3
DECONSTRUCTION FOR BEGINNERS:	ISBN 978-1-934389-26-3
DEMOCRACY FOR BEGINNERS:	ISBN 978-1-934389-36-2
DERRIDA FOR BEGINNERS:	ISBN 978-1-934389-11-9
EASTERN PHILOSOPHY FOR BEGINNERS:	ISBN 978-1-934389-07-2
EXISTENTIALISM FOR BEGINNERS:	ISBN 978-1-934389-21-8
FOUCAULT FOR BEGINNERS:	ISBN 978-1-934389-12-6
GLOBAL WARMING FOR BEGINNERS:	ISBN 978-1-934389-27-0
HEIDEGGER FOR BEGINNERS:	ISBN 978-1-934389-13-3
ISLAM FOR BEGINNERS:	ISBN 978-1-934389-01-0
KIERKEGAARD FOR BEGINNERS:	ISBN 978-1-934389-14-0
LINGUISTICS FOR BEGINNERS:	ISBN 978-1-934389-28-7
MALCOLM X FOR BEGINNERS:	ISBN 978-1-934389-04-1
NIETZSCHE FOR BEGINNERS:	ISBN 978-1-934389-05-8
THE OLYMPICS FOR BEGINNERS:	ISBN 978-1-934389-33-1
PHILOSOPHY FOR BEGINNERS:	ISBN 978-1-934389-02-7
PLATO FOR BEGINNERS:	ISBN 978-1-934389-08-9
POSTMODERNISM FOR BEGINNERS:	ISBN 978-1-934389-09-6
SARTRE FOR BEGINNERS:	ISBN 978-1-934389-15-7
SHAKESPEARE FOR BEGINNERS:	ISBN 978-1-934389-29-4
STRUCTURALISM & POSTSTRUCTURALISM FOR BEGINNERS:	ISBN 978-1-934389-10-2
ZEN FOR BEGINNERS:	ISBN 978-1-934389-06-5

www.forbeginnersbooks.com